Conducting the
in Child Protect

D0715537

Conducting the Home Visit in Child Protection

Joanna Nicolas

Open University Press

Open University Press
McGraw-Hill Education
McGraw-Hill House
Shoppenhangers Road
Maidenhead
Berkshire
England
SL6 2QL

email: enquiries@openup.co.uk
world wide web: www.openup.co.uk

and Two Penn Plaza, New York, NY 10121-2289, USA

First published 2012

A catalogue record of this book is available from the British Library

ISBN-13: 978-0-33 524527-7 (pb)
ISBN-10: 0-33-524527-7 (pb)
eISBN: 978-0-33-524528-4

Library of Congress Cataloging-in-Publication Data
CIP data applied for

Typesetting and e-book compilations by
RefineCatch Limited, Bungay, Suffolk
Printed and bound by CPI Group (UK) Ltd, Croydon, CR0 4YY

The *McGraw·Hill* Companies

'For anyone immersed in child protection, there is a requirement to be aware, alert and assertive and to be inquisitive, intrigued, inquiring and imaginative about what children are experiencing when you are not there. These are the powerful messages from this strongly practice-focussed text with its emphasis on "how to do it". There is clear guidance, and powerful examples, for those still learning their craft and significant reminders for those who are more experienced. There is no more important work than protecting very vulnerable children. This book will help us all do it better.'

Ray Jones, Professor of Social Work, Kingston University and St George's, University of London, UK and previously Director of Social Services in Wiltshire, UK

'This is an immensely readable and engaging book, which would have been an enormous resource for me as a practitioner and as a manager of social workers, earlier on in my career. It is written in a succinct, authentic, and clear style with practical examples throughout . . . Joanna Nicolas brings her commitment to learning from practice alive in this book, drawing on personal examples. Her clarity on issues, such as the legal position of social workers, is excellent.'

Penny Thompson, Chief Executive of the General Social Care Council (GSCC)

'This book is a gem. Filled with numerous practice-based examples and laced with contemporary, "real-world" dilemmas, it gently encourages practitioners involved in child protection work to think about their work. Whatever their level of knowledge and experience, this book offers excellent, hands-on advice from someone who, clearly, has much experience with families. But what Joanna Nicolas also brings is humanity and a real concern for people: no mean achievement!'

David Shemmings PhD, Professor of Child Protection Research, University of Kent and Royal Holloway, University of London, UK

Contents

How to use this book

This pocket book is designed to help guide you through the process of visiting families in their homes in cases of child protection. The book can be dipped into and out as needed, it does not have to be read from cover to cover and provides a range of complementary yet stand-alone aspects of conducting the home visit.

This is an extremely practical guide and some chapters will include check-lists such as how to prepare for a visit, what to take on the visit, how to make the most of your visit and how to keep yourself safe. There will be examples of good and poor practice, case examples drawn from my own experience and that of others, and quick links to research.

Chapter 1 sets out what needs to be done in preparation for a visit. It is essential to be well prepared before you visit someone's home and the reasons for this are made clear in this chapter.

Chapter 2 looks at how to actually gain access to the home. You may wonder why you need a chapter on this topic but obtaining entry can be a tricky part of a visit and this chapter will give you tips and advice on how to be successful in this.

Chapter 3 sets out what you need to do once you are in the home. It will help you consider where to place yourself in a room, where you should be going in the home, who you need to talk to, all of this while emphasizing the need to keep the child as the focus of why you are there.

Chapter 4 gives guidance on what to look out for in the home, i.e. the possible signs of abuse or neglect. What is the state of the home? How does the child present, the adults present, and how do the two interact? The chapter stresses the need to use your observational skills. This is where they are key.

Chapter 5 gives tips and guidance on keeping yourself safe when conducting a home visit. Personal safety must always be a priority when conducting a home visit and should never be forgotten. Use your common sense in this situation.

Further reading and resources can be found at the back of the book to help maintain and develop your practice. These consider both your overall knowledge base and your specific report writing skills. They are intended to give you some initial signposts to further reading and resources that can be accessed.

There is also a glossary, and glossary terms are shown in bold on their first occurrence. The use of jargon in this book is kept to a minimum but there is some professional terminology that needs to be understood. These terms are explained in the glossary but it also goes further than that. The glossary also sets out and explains legal terms and common themes found in child protection.

The overall aim of this book is to provide you with a flexible and accessible resource that can help you when you are conducting home visits.

Acknowledgements

This book is dedicated to my mother, who is the most exceptional person I know. Without her unwavering love, support, interest and encouragement I would not be in the position I am today. I must also thank my beloved husband and children for putting up with me, and the friends and colleagues who have supported and encouraged me in this project, in particular, Rebecca Kay, James Lovell, Jane Bee and Mark Little. Thank you all.

Introduction

This is a book for social workers and other professionals who visit homes in difficult circumstances. I write this book as a social worker but there are many other professionals who have to visit people's homes and this can be very challenging work. Therefore, this book is for all the social workers, health visitors, community family workers, education welfare workers, teachers and anyone else who is responsible for the welfare of children.

I was delighted to be asked to write it because a practical guide of what to do on a home visit has not been written previously. As a student and a newly qualified social worker I would have benefited greatly from a practical guide in a book like this, something I could keep in my bag. At university I learnt the theories, I studied the research but little practical guidance was given. What do you do when you go to visit a family for the first time, and you knock on the door, the door opens and you smile warmly and say, 'Hello, I'm Joanna Nicolas, and I am a social worker' and the response is to be sworn at and the door slammed in your face?

But this book is not just for newly qualified staff. If you are a student or newly qualified worker, this book will complement and supplement the theories you have learnt, improve your study and will help you turn theory into practice. It can also be used by more experienced practitioners, as it will consolidate what you do in your practice. Life is a continuing learning process and if anyone thinks they know it all, I would question their practice. We should all be learning all the time.

> ### ✓ Good Practice Point: We Never Know It All
>
> At one point in my career I had a five-year career break, to have my children. The first meeting I attended on my return was a child protection conference. There was no family member present and during the meeting a drugs worker was telling the conference about all the different drugs the mother in the family was using. The worker went through a long list which included heroin, methadone, crack-cocaine, etc. and ended with 'Tudor Rose'. There were about 15 professionals at that meeting and they were all shaking their heads at the gravity of the situation. All I could think was that I did not know what Tudor Rose was – was it a new drug that had come on the market while I had been away? If I owned up to my ignorance, would it be like saying I did not know what methadone was? Eventually I had to ask and the drugs worker looked at me as if I really should not have been there, if I knew so little. Witheringly, she told me it was sherry. Looking round at the other professionals it was clear that none of them had the first idea what Tudor Rose was but no one wanted to show their lack of knowledge. Tudor Rose is extremely affordable sherry, and I did not feel so bad I did not know!

The reason for this good practice point is to emphasise that we never 'know it all'. We should never be afraid to ask questions, whether of the families we work with, or of our colleagues. We can all learn, and I hope that this book will help all of you, regardless of your years of experience, to improve your practice, question it if necessary and most importantly assist you in the difficult work that you do.

Throughout this book, case examples and good practice points are included. The race and gender of the parents and the children, as well as the age of the children, have been changed to ensure complete privacy for the families and children I have met in the 21 years I have worked in social care, in this country and abroad. Other details have also been changed.

Carrying out home visits is one of the hardest areas of social work. However, it is where most assessments of whether a child is safe should take place. The most significant aspect of a child protection investigation will take place in the family home and yet it can be the most challenging and hostile environment to work in. It is also the place where we find out the most about the child. It is unsurprising that child abuse inquiries report that the evidence is often before the social worker's eyes, when they are in a family home. We just have to know where to look and what to do. As Ferguson (2009) observes, in some of our most high profile child deaths, Jasmine Beckford (London Borough of Brent 1985), Victoria Climbié[1] and Peter Connelly,[2] the signs were there but they were missed. Five-year-old Jasmine Beckford was seen by a social worker during a home visit but she was watching television and only stood up when her mother and the social worker entered the room. The social worker was in the room for 20 minutes and described Jasmine and her sisters as 'well and happy'. We now know that at that time Jasmine was recovering from a fracture to her thigh. Jasmine was battered to death by her step-father Maurice Beckford on 5 July 1984. She had been locked in a bedroom with body-building weights tied to her broken legs to stop her moving. When she died, she was emaciated and deformed, she weighed just 23 pounds. She had 40 injuries to her face and body – her ribs were also broken and she had ulcers, burns and cuts to her leg.

In the case of Victoria Climbié, there was one occasion on which a social worker did a home visit. Victoria was sitting on the floor throughout the visit. The social worker's recording said that Victoria was clean, well-dressed and playing with a doll. That was the time Victoria was kept tied up in the bath. She was doubly incontinent because she was so frightened and she was kept in a bin bag because of her incontinence. The reason why she was sitting on the floor during the visit was because she could not stand up straight, as most of the time she was tied up. Victoria died of hypothermia because the bathroom she was kept in was freezing. She had 128 injuries on her body when she died on 25 February 2000.

In the case of Peter Connelly, it is well documented that a considerable number of home visits were done by social workers and other professionals. It was noted that the home was in a poor state, that Peter often had bruises and on one occasion his face was smeared with chocolate and he had cream on his head. During that visit it is understood the social worker asked the mother to clean his face, a friend took him out of the room but did not return him. Those home visits could certainly have been put to better use in the efforts to protect Peter. He had more than 50 injuries on his body when he died on 3 August 200⁻

These are just three of the terrible tragedies that have occurred when a child has died of **abuse** or **neglect**. As these cases highlight, the signs were there. There is a myth that children who are horrifically abused and neglected are hidden away, unknown to us all. That is untrue. Almost all are known to universal services, i.e. Health Services and/or Education Services, and around half are known to **social care**. This is the evidence that comes from the analysis of serious case reviews[3] undertaken on behalf of the UK government (Brandon et al. 2009). This book will help you consider what the signs are, the significance of what is happening in the home, the importance of seeing the whole home, the whole family, and the importance of observing the child within the family context.

The aim of this book is to help you in what is the most essential part of our work, to gain the most from your home visit. Of course, not every family we visit will be hostile, not every home will have an aggressive dog, but a significant number of families we visit will not want us there. This book will address all aspects of the home visit. We can learn so much from visiting the home and it is vital that we use our skills to the best of our ability. A spotless house and a bulging toy cupboard do not mean there is no risk of neglect, just as a dirty house and a mountain of washing-up do not mean there must be neglect. This book will challenge assumptions, prejudices and stereotypes. The aim is to give you the tools to assess and challenge the families we work with, regardless of the family's social status.

Example from Practice

Many years ago, as a social worker on duty, I was given the unenviable task of contacting a parent, whose child was being collected from primary school every day by a babysitter. It had come to social care's attention that the babysitter was taking the child to a pub every day and the babysitter was then drinking heavily and not supervising the child, who would wander around the pub. Clearly there were concerns about this child.

However, the parent did not respond to a letter from social care, so I telephoned the home. The parent could barely contain their fury and disgust that they, an eminent professional, which they were, were being contacted by a mere social worker. The parent made it clear they thought it was absolutely none of our business what arrangements they made for their child despite my insistence it was a child protection concern and therefore it was most definitely our business. The parent refused to discuss it further, and the case was closed, after the referrer was asked to come back to us if this continued. Would social care's response have been different if the family had been disadvantaged and unemployed?

This book will help you to work through the anxieties you may have. It will help you to find ways of dealing with possible hostility, as well as coping with the pressures of work and time. Ultimately, it will help put you in control. This book will give you the tools to use to establish yourself when you are visiting a family, so you are able to adopt a position of reasonable and non-hostile authority. You are there to do a job but you are also in their home. Social workers must be authoritative without being authoritarian. We are there to listen and to observe. If there ever was a time for social workers to be saying to their managers that they need to invest the time in a family, it is now. Professor Munro (2010, 2011) has highlighted the need for social workers to have greater autonomy and the need for social workers to spend more time with families, assessing risk. Yet at the same time we have to be realistic about the pressures of work, and the aim of this book is to ensure that you make the most of the limited time you have on a home visit.

We live in a world dominated by political correctness. The sadness is, the motivation for political correctness is entirely right – to end discrimination of any kind and yet, as often happens, it has been hijacked by extremists and has come to be ridiculed by many. So when I make the disclaimer that this is not a 'politically correct' book, of course I do not mean I believe in discrimination, but common sense must prevail.

For example, if a teacher hears of a young Muslim girl who is going to be taken back to her country of origin to be genitally mutilated, the teacher must act. (Apart from the child protection aspect, female genital mutilation is a criminal offence and under the Female Genital Mutilation Act, 2003, it is now a criminal act to plan to take a child out of the UK for her to be mutilated.) A White, British teacher may be afraid to report it because they do not want to be seen to be racist. We must not lose our focus on what the priority is – children's safety and well-being. That is the focus in this book and the methods recommended here put the child and not the need to be politically correct at the centre of practice. We must not confuse political correctness with cultural sensitivity.

This book is also 'jargon-free'. We are all guilty of using jargon and often use it as a protective mechanism when we are feeling defensive. I will never forget as a newly qualified social worker visiting a parent, with an experienced social worker. The parent was a chronic alcoholic and the children were young and unsupervised much of the time. When we arrived, the parent was slumped in a chair, eyes half-closed, bottle in hand. The senior social worker stood at the door and said to the parent, 'If you don't do something about your drinking, we are going to have to initiate child protection proceedings.' The parent stared at her, with eyes crossed. I struggled to understand what those words meant and I was qualified as a social worker. The parent obviously did not understand. We must beware of jargon.

In this introduction I must own up to my personal bugbear: the use of the words 'appropriate' and 'inappropriate'. They are words that we use all the time that cover a multitude of meanings, so they now are meaningless. If you are visiting someone's house and you tell them you are concerned about their child's inappropriate behaviour, what does that mean? I hope that you will start to notice how often these words come up and how little they mean. What is 'inappropriate sexualised behaviour'? What is 'inappropriate language'? Context and culture are important here.

Example from Practice

I was working with a primary school child who had exhibited 'inappropriate sexualised behaviour', according to the school. The school had told the parent about their concerns over this behaviour. The parent did not know what the school meant. Actually what the child was doing was asking teachers if they were virgins. The child was touching teachers' breasts and bottoms and using every possible object as a phallic object. That tells you about this child's behaviour, not the blanket statement 'inappropriate sexualised behaviour'.

Before we move on to the main body of the book, here is just a gentle reminder about the position of power we are in when we knock on someone's door, and then when we enter someone's home. It may not feel like it sometimes but we should put ourselves in the family's position. Social workers in particular have considerable powers and we know that the public's perception is that social workers take children away. We can change families' lives, and whether it is a child protection investigation or an assessment of potential adopters, never underestimate the position of power we are in. That power must not be abused but at the same time we must not allow ourselves to be intimidated into thinking we are powerless.

So let's remind ourselves why we do this job. Sometimes children need protecting and that is what we are there for. What could be more important than the protection of the most vulnerable in our society? I am proud to call myself a social worker and I am proud of my profession, even if the only time the general public hear about us is when there has been a terrible tragedy involving a child. It is right that we, as a profession, do not retaliate. Our priority must always be the family we are working with, with the child at the centre. We must hold our hands up when our failings have contributed to the death of a child and we must learn from it. We must also bear it when we are unjustly accused because our priority must be the child.

Example from Practice

I once heard a mother I had worked with tell her friend that social care had taken her child away because she was epileptic. She also went to the press and this was reported in the papers. Inevitably and understandably because of that information, social workers were heavily criticised for being so cruel. Aside from the fact that social workers do not have the power to remove children, only the police and the courts can do so, this woman's child had been removed from her care because she was an intravenous drug user who prostituted herself to pay for her drugs and used to take her clients back to her bedsit where she would have sex with them in front of her young child. That was the reason her child had been removed from her care but what purpose would it have served to have gone to the press with that? Yes, it would have shown social workers in a better light but this woman was so vulnerable and was a victim of her circumstances. She had

> been sexually abused as a child. Most of the families we work with are very vulnerable and it is easy to take advantage of that vulnerability.

We must ensure we do the best job we possibly can, in whatever circumstances we find ourselves and focus on what matters, the protection of children. My aim is that this book will help you do that.

1 **Preparing for the visit**

It is all too common for a worker to be ill prepared for a visit. Take control. You are a professional there to do a job. It is your responsibility to ensure you are prepared. What is the purpose of your visit? What do you hope to achieve from the visit? What factual information do you require? What information do you already have?

This chapter will look at the vital preparation necessary to get the most from the home visit, even if all that means is sitting in your car for five minutes composing yourself before you go in. You will find that time spent in preparation saves time later on and it will also ensure you get the most from the visit. Use the checklist on p. 22 to tick off what you have done in preparation. Whether you are a beginner, or an experienced worker, there is no doubt that the more organised and better prepared we are, the more time-efficient we can be. That can only be a good thing.

WHAT TYPE OF VISIT IS IT?

There are different considerations, depending on what type of visit it is. This chapter will look at the different types of visits and what needs to be done in preparation for each one. We will focus primarily on arranging the initial visit, but will also be considering the importance of unannounced visits.

■ *The initial visit.* You will need to consider how best to arrange the visit, does the family speak English? Are they literate? Should you telephone to arrange the visit? Are there safety issues you need to be aware of? What is the purpose of the visit?
■ *The joint visit.* We do joint visits for a number of reasons. It may be that there are safety issues and it is thought unwise to visit alone or because you want a second opinion on what you have previously witnessed in the

home. It may be that you are visiting with the police, who are going to arrest someone and you are there to ensure the children's safety and well-being. Or you and another agency have decided a joint visit would be beneficial, for any number of reasons. Perhaps you are going to be discussing something very painful for the primary carer and it is thought to be important for them to have some support.

■ *A follow-up visit.* When you do your initial visit, it is important to establish the best way of arranging visits with the family in future in terms of how you make contact with them, whether there will be an interpreter present, who will read any reports if the family is not literate. You will also need to think about whether future visits should be with another worker, if you are concerned about your safety. This should be discussed with your manager. You will also need to be clear about the purpose of future visits. What are you there to do and what do you need from subsequent visits? (It is too easy to 'do a visit' to tick the box saying you have done the statutory or mandatory visit but you need to think why you are there.)

■ *An unannounced visit.* There are situations which merit an unannounced visit. It may be necessary if we believe a family is being dishonest with us about who is in the home, who is caring for the children, whether someone in the home is misusing substances, etc.

Regardless of what kind of visit it is, you need to think ahead and be well organised.

THE INITIAL VISIT: GETTING IN TOUCH WITH THE FAMILY

First of all, what is the best way of getting in touch with the family? Is it better to write a letter and put it in the post, or drop it off yourself? (The advantage of dropping the letter off yourself is that you know it arrived at the home, which is always helpful if a family denies receiving a letter.) Or is it better to telephone the family? We can only decide on the best way to contact a family once we have considered the following factors:

■ *Does the family have a history of avoiding contact with social care?* If we know the family is good at avoiding social care, and if we write a letter and post it and the family denies receiving that letter, there is no proof they did so. Therefore, it would be better to drop the letter in personally, or telephone. That way you have evidence you did make contact.

■ *Does the family speak English?* The person who made the referral should be able to tell you that. If they do not speak English, or only the children do, then it would be best to contact them by letter and the letter must be in the family's own language.[1]

■ *Do you need an interpreter?* You may need to arrange for a letter to be translated and you may need to arrange for an interpreter to accompany you on your visit. If you need to use either service, make sure the person you use is from a professional body, not a helpful neighbour.

Good Practice Point: Poor Practice

I was once working with a family who was Japanese. There were considerable concerns that the children were neglected and physically uncared for. The mother's English was very limited and we had some difficulty finding an interpreter. Eventually I came across a voluntary organisation that said they could offer us a service.

During my first visit with the interpreter, I soon realised that something was amiss. Now my Japanese is not impressive but I started noticing that for every sentence I said, the interpreter would 'translate' longer, for several minutes. Eventually I realised that he was translating and then commenting on what I was saying and adding his own opinion about the mother's neglect of the children. Of course, I could not continue and I came away from that house knowing that I had added to this mother's troubles because I had brought someone into her home from her own community and had shared with them some intimate details about her difficulties.

That is an example of very poor practice, which I am ashamed of, but have never repeated.

■ *Is the family literate?* Again, check if the referrer knows, or other agencies involved with the family. If you know the family is literate, you can then make the decision on whether it is best to write, or telephone to arrange the visit, based on the other factors. If you know the family is illiterate, then you will need to telephone to arrange the visit.

■ *Does the family know a referral was made to social care?* social care should be checking this with the referrer and advising them that unless it will result in making someone unsafe, the referrer should tell the family they are making the referral. If the family knows a referral has been made, they will be waiting for you to contact them. There may be situations where it is decided it would not be safe to tell a family a referral has been made to social care. For example, if a 6-year-old girl arrives at school, clearly in pain and tells a teacher that her father has put his willy in her bottom, there is blood in her underwear and it appears she may have been raped. In that situation the school would definitely not tell the parents that they were making a referral to social care. For all the agencies, the work we do is about protecting children and ensuring their safety. For the police it is also about securing evidence, if it is thought someone has committed an offence. In that situation the school would make a referral to social care immediately and advise them that they had not told the parents they had made the referral. At the subsequent **strategy discussion** it would be decided how the family was to be approached.

■ *Is there evidence of an abusive relationship and are you going to put anyone at risk by writing a letter?* As part of any assessment social care needs to ask other relevant agencies if this is the case. If there is domestic abuse and a domestic abuse agency is involved, it is best to take advice from them about how to contact the non-violent partner. For you, the worker, it is your responsibility to check this out.

■ *Does anyone in the family have learning difficulties, or a disability that you need to be aware of?* Again, check with other agencies who have been involved. If, for example, the primary carer is deaf, you may need to take someone with you who can sign.

Example from Practice

A referral had come in from the probation service. It concerned a single child under the age of 5, living with their mother and father. The father was extremely violent and had a recent conviction for assaulting his partner, with whom he and the child lived. There was a long history of domestic abuse. It was agreed in the first instance that I should meet with the mother, to ascertain and assess the situation. We would then decide how best to incorporate the father in the assessment we were doing. I was concerned about writing to the mother, or telephoning her, in case her partner saw the letter, or listened to the call. I knew that the mother had contact with a local domestic abuse support group and so I contacted them for advice. The support group had devised a way to contact the mother safely and I followed the same procedure. This ensured the mother's and the child's safety, which was of course the priority.

(In the interests of protecting the vulnerable adults and children we work with, I have deliberately not spelt out the method used.)

We need to take all these factors into consideration when deciding how to make contact with a family to arrange a visit. Once you have the information, you can then decide how best to proceed.

Writing the Letter to Arrange the Visit

If you have decided to write a letter, use plain English (if that is the language you are using). Do not use jargon and please do not use the words 'appropriate' or 'inappropriate'!

Example of a Standard Letter

Date

Dear X,

I am writing to you because, as you know, Mary's school has some worries about her, and James's health visitor is a bit concerned that James is not putting on weight. I would like to come and see you to talk about this and wondered if I could come on . . . at . . .? If that time does not suit you, please would you telephone me on . . . so that we can make another appointment?

Please note that it is important that I come and see you. There may be ways that social care or other agencies can offer you support. At the meeting I will explain to you what the role of social care is.

I look forward to meeting you.

Regards,

So the message is, *keep it simple.* I would not go into too much detail in a letter and I would definitely not give reassurance that there is nothing to be worried about, because that may be misleading for the parent. It is one of the dilemmas we have. We ask families to be honest and open with us and then when they are, it sometimes results in us having to remove a child or children after a decision is made by the Court.

Arranging the Visit by Telephone

You may have been told that the family is illiterate and in that case you should telephone the family to arrange the visit. (It would not be fair to write a letter to a family, knowing they were not able to read it. They may well show it to someone who is able to read it to them and that person then knows their private business.)

Example of a Telephone Call to Arrange an Initial Visit

You: Hello. Could I please speak to X? (Use first name and second name.)

Service user: Who is it?

You: My name is Joanna. Is X there? (Or if it is a mobile, 'Is that X?')
(Do not give more than a first name until you have established who you are speaking to. Nor should you say where you are calling from, until you know you are speaking to the service user.)

Service user: So what if it is?

You: I'm sorry but I really need to know who I am speaking to before I explain why I am calling. Is that X?

Service user: Yeah.

(You need to decide how you are going to address them. You will not know if that person would prefer to be addressed formally, or by their first name. We should not presume to call someone by their first name, unless we have asked if we can do so. I would therefore suggest that in most cases you address the person as Mr/Mrs/Ms.)

You: OK. My name is Joanna Nicolas and I am a social worker. I work for ... The reason why I am calling you is because I would like to arrange to come and see you to talk about Mary and James. As you know, the health visitor and the school have been a bit worried about the children and I just need to come and see you, to talk about it and also to see whether there is anything we can do to help.

Service user: I don't need any help from you.

You: That is fine but I do need to come and see you because the school and the health visitor have passed on their concerns to us and so a social worker has to come and see you and the children. I was wondering whether I could come on ... at ...?

Service user: I don't want anyone coming round. You are not taking my children off me.

You: Ms X, I am not coming round to take your children away but I do need to come and see you. Now, what about ...?

Service user: Why can't we do it over the phone?

You: Because I need to come and see you at home and talk to you and see the children. Now, what days are best for you?

Service user: I can't do Mondays.

You: That's absolutely fine. What about Tuesday at 4 p.m.?

Service user: If you must.

You: Thank you. Now what I will do is send you a text with my name and number and when I am coming to see you. If there are any problems, please would you give me a ring and let me know? Thank you for your time, Ms X, and I look forward to seeing you on Tuesday at 4 p.m.

There are different levels of literacy and therefore send a simple text with the date and time and your name.

Again, keep it simple, just as you would with a letter. Keep the conversation quite brief. Do not allow yourself to be drawn into talking about the concerns on the telephone. Take control of the conversation, be courteous but firm.

You need to arrange a date and a time to suit you both but if you feel the service-user is prevaricating, take control.

If the service user puts the telephone down on you and then switches their telephone off, you will need to let your manager know you have been unable to reach them and decide on the next course of action.

Gathering the Information You Need

- *Does the referrer know you are contacting the family?* Again, social care should have made it clear to the referrer what is going to happen next, and whether social care is going to visit the family. If you are the worker doing the first assessment, it is your responsibility to let the referrer know what is happening.
- *Is there a potential risk to you?* This is one of the reasons why it is essential to read the file. Is there any evidence that anyone in the home is potentially violent? This must be considered in light of the subject you will be discussing with the family. Should you be visiting alone? Should you be visiting the home at all? You need to weigh up the risks. Unless the situation is so grave that social care are going to seek an emergency protection order or the police are going to take the child into police protection, seeing the child in the home is an essential aspect of any assessment of risk. However, this must be balanced against the potential risk to you. What you need to consider is that if workers are unwilling to go into a home because of concerns for their own safety, how can it be a safe place for a child to be?
- *What do we mean when we talk about 'doing a risk assessment'?* In this context we are talking about whether it is safe for you to visit the home. This book is about child protection and therefore the police will have been involved in the strategy discussion. You need to know before you do a visit, whether the family is known to the police and whether there are any concerns relevant to your visit, such as violent assaults, or drug dealing from the property. If you have concerns, these should be discussed with your manager. You should always be looking to minimise risk, while

accepting that it is vital to see a child in their own environment. It may be that taking another worker with you reduces the risk. If you are visiting alone, make sure you have a mobile with you and if you need to, have it on but keep it on silent. It is your responsibility to ensure your employer knows of your whereabouts.

Reminder Box: Official Policy on Lone Working

Different employers have different policies on lone working and staff safety. As a general rule, if you are concerned about your safety, discuss it with your manager.

Example from Practice

I once had to meet with a father, whose partner had recently left him due to the high level of violence. She had gone into a refuge in another area. All this happened without his knowledge because of his threats to kill his partner and his child if she ever left him. These threats were taken extremely seriously, particularly in view of his history of violence and substance abuse.

As the children's social worker I had to tell the father that social care was going to apply to the Court for an **interim care order** for the child and we were going to recommend to the Court that he only have contact with the child, supervised by a social worker.

In view of what I was going to be telling him and his history of violence, it would clearly be unsafe to visit him where he was living at the time. It was agreed I would see him in a neutral venue, with a colleague and with police back-up, in case he became violent. The police officers were not visible but it was reassuring to know they were there, if need be.

■ *Read the file.* This is essential. Time will always be an issue for us but if you visit someone's house and you have not read the file, you may have missed some essential information that may impact on your safety, as well as the child's. If there is a lot of information on the file, skim read it. Pick out the essential assessments, reports, etc.

■ *Speak to other agencies.* Best practice would dictate that you speak to all the other agencies involved before you visit. This may not be practicable and in any case if you are doing a child protection investigation, there will already have been a strategy discussion. If you did not attend that discussion, make sure you have read the minutes, or at the very least spoken to the manager who attended.

■ *Speak to the previous worker.* If you are taking the case over from another social worker, ask them if there is anything you should be aware of before you visit. This can also be done with other workers, for example, the health visitor.

■ *Do you need to take any paperwork with you?* Again, when you are thinking about the purpose of your visit, you should be thinking about paperwork. Are there papers/reports to be read and signed by the family?

■ *Race/ethnicity/cultural issues.* You need to be well prepared. We have already looked at language but culture is also essential. In this chapter we are only looking at the preparation we need to do before a visit. Therefore, at this point we are only considering cultural issues in that context. It is common courtesy that we find out what we can about the culture of the family before we visit, so we do not offend. It is also helpful to know for ourselves, so we are prepared. It is not possible to generalise about any ethnic group and therefore it is good advice to mention this aspect when you are asking a previous worker or a worker from another agency, whether there is anything you need to be aware of.

■ *What will you wear?* What you wear is very relevant and should be considered. It is important to remember that we are professionals and there to do a job, so we need to look professional if we want to be respected. But we must also be practical about it and if, for example, you are going to a house where there are small children, you may well be climbed on or find yourself sitting on the floor, so better not to wear a short skirt. It is very important that we do everything in our power to put the families at their ease but if, as is so often the case, it is not just the child who is neglected but also the home, it's hard to appear relaxed about sinking into a sofa with a seat decorated with squashed jammy dodgers, spilt juice and dog hairs if you are wearing your new suit which is 'Dry Clean Only'. A colleague of mine recently found herself removing a hypodermic needle before she could sit down. So wear things you can throw in the wash when you get home and then you can relax and concentrate on what really matters – the child.

Example from Practice

Some of my most embarrassing visits have been when I have been wearing a skirt and boots and I am asked if I would mind taking off my boots. I have a terrible sinking feeling because I realise that I left home in an awful hurry that morning and it suddenly dawns on me I am wearing my son's Star Wars socks. It would be quite wrong to refuse to take my boots off so I sit there talking about child abuse with bare legs and Star Wars socks. It is not very professional and can somewhat undermine one's authority. I would find it quite hard to take that person seriously. (The same applies if you are wearing tights with a hole or ladder in them.) Keep a spare pair of tights or socks in the car. We have to think of everything!

JOINT VISITS

If you are doing a joint visit with a colleague from your own profession, or another, you need to be clear before you enter the home about your individual roles. If you are unable to have a conversation before you leave the office, the very least you should do is arrange to meet ten minutes beforehand and talk through the purpose of the visit and your roles. (I would suggest you do not park outside the home you are going to. It may be unnerving for the service user to see you both sitting and talking before the visit and if the family sees you and does have something to hide, you are giving them the opportunity to prepare.) If professionals are unprepared and disorganised a manipulative service user will use that to play professionals off against each other.

Good Practice Point: Working with Other Professionals

I worked with a mother who appeared to be cooperating with professionals. Her children were subject to child protection plans because of concerns the children were being neglected. Part of the child protection plan was that the mother would attend the baby clinic once a week, to have her baby weighed, this was an area of concern. It was during a conversation in the health visitor's car, just before we did a joint visit, that we realised that the mother was playing one of us off against the other, telling each of us that the other had said that she need no longer take her baby to be weighed. This alerted us, and the other professionals involved, to the fact that she was an extremely manipulative woman and we must therefore work very closely together.

UNANNOUNCED VISITS

Unannounced visits are an essential part of the child protection process. We need to be clear why we consider it necessary with any particular family. I know how I would feel if a professional arrived on my doorstep without warning. (I would always try at least to tidy up when the health visitor was coming. With my first baby, it was an achievement if I was dressed and had done the washing up by 11 a.m.)

Having said that, we can learn so much from unannounced visits. In the second serious case review in the case of Peter Connelly, the review states, 'The value of an unannounced visit by the social worker was demonstrated in bringing the injuries to Peter to light.'[2]

Good Practice Point: Follow Your Hunch

There are so many examples but this is one that remains with me.

I was involved in a private law case. Both parents wanted custody of the two children and both said the other was an unfit parent. The judge had ordered the parents share the care of the children. Both parents would go into great detail about the other's poor parenting but there was little evidence of this. The father would tell me the mother was a heavy drinker but every time I visited there was no evidence of this. The home was always immaculate and the children appeared loved and well cared for. The mother was always welcoming and courteous.

The mother had a full-time job and so my visits were always by appointment. One day, on a hunch, I decided to do an unannounced visit in the early evening. The mother did not see who it was before she opened the door. She was clearly drunk, the house was in disarray and there was no sign of the children. When I asked where they were, she told me they were in their rooms and she would get them. She started going upstairs and I followed her saying blithely, 'I'll just come with you, if you don't mind. It would be nice to see them in their rooms.' She gave me a filthy look, which I just ignored and carried on smiling. (You have to be very thick-skinned to be a social worker!) There was little she could do, without appearing impolite and she did not want to spoil the façade she had built up from the beginning. When we got to the bedrooms, there were keys in the doors and the children had been locked in.

What is a hunch? Professionals often talk about having 'a hunch', or instinctively knowing something. Quite rightly, we need evidence of abuse but as our experience builds up, so does our expertise. It is the opinion of Duncan Helm, a social work professor at the University of Stirling, (and of many others) that child protection workers should be encouraged to rely more on gut instincts and intuition.

The second point to make is that I felt entirely safe with this woman, in this house. I would never recommend doing what I did if any part of me felt unsafe.

Undoubtedly we will learn more from an unannounced visit and while it would be wrong to encourage workers to be devious, if there are concerns about who is in the home, or visiting the home, it may be worth stepping aside when you have rung the bell and not being in full view before the door is answered. In the case of Peter Connelly, professionals were unaware of who was living in the home and yet Peter and his two siblings were subject to child protection plans, considered to be at risk of physical abuse and neglect. Following Peter's death, his mother Tracy Connelly, her boyfriend Steven Barker and her lodger, Mr Barker's brother, Jason Owen were all convicted of causing or allowing the death of a child. All had been living in the house, along with Mr Owen's girlfriend and his children.

✓

Good Practice Checklist

Things to Take with You on the Visit

- ✓ Pen and paper
- ✓ Diary
- ✓ Mobile (with battery charged)
- ✓ If there are specific questions for the family it is helpful to have those written down, so you can be sure you have asked them. Is there any paperwork you need to take?

Checklist of Things to Do in Preparation

- ✓ Read the file.
- ✓ Speak to other agencies.
- ✓ Speak to previous workers.
- ✓ Do an assessment of risk.
- ✓ Make sure the relevant person in your team knows where you are going and what time you will be back. See Chapter 5 on personal safety.
- ✓ Telephone the family to confirm the appointment. Be friendly; say you are looking forward to seeing them, or something similar.
- ✓ If you are doing a joint visit, make a plan with your co-visitor before you go.
- ✓ Be clear in your mind about the purpose of your visit.
- ✓ Find out if there are any racial/ethnicity/cultural issues, such as language.

Hopefully this chapter has persuaded you of the need to be prepared, however little time you have. If you forget to take the paperwork, you will have to go back and that will take more time. If you were in such a rush, you did not remember to ask an essential question you may have to go back. However much pressure we are under, ultimately we are all responsible for our own conduct. Part of being a professional is recognising one's own capabilities and limitations and acknowledging these with our managers. The manager may not be able to decrease your workload but he or she may be able to help you to better manage your time. And at least the situation will have been acknowledged and recorded. You will achieve better results and feel so much better if you are in control.

2 Getting in the Door

We have to be aware that many of the families we visit do not want us there. For many families their greatest concern will be that we are going to take their children away and therefore physically getting in through the door may not be as straightforward as it seems.

Point of Law: Removal of Children from Their Parents/Carers

Only the police and the courts have the legal power to remove children from their parents/carers. The police can take a child into police protection if they have 'reasonable cause to believe' that the child would otherwise suffer significant harm (s.46, Children Act, 1989). This protection lasts for 72 hours; otherwise social care would apply to the Court for an emergency protection order (s.44, Children Act, 1989). An emergency protection order lasts for eight days and can be extended for a further seven days. If it is not deemed to be an emergency, social care would apply to the Court for an interim care order (s.38, Children Act, 1989). An interim care order will last for eight weeks and will then have to be renewed.

SOCIAL WORKERS DO NOT HAVE THE LEGAL POWER TO REMOVE CHILDREN.

This chapter will look at what to do when the family allows us in and what to do when the family is hostile and tells us to go away. It is important to bear in mind that the family that welcomes us with open arms is not necessarily the one that is treating its children well and the family that is hostile and resistant is not necessarily the one that is abusing its children.

In your preparation for the visit you should have been able to ascertain whether there are any issues of personal safety to consider and planned accordingly (see Chapter 1). If the family is known to other agencies, you may have some idea as to whether they are generally amenable to working with professionals, though when faced with professionals working in child protection, the reaction may be very different. Any information you have should affect how you actually physically approach the property.

Good Practice Box: General Guidance

- When the door is opened, only give your first name, until you have established who you are speaking to. Then ask for the full name of the person you are there to see.
- When the door is answered, always give the first and second name of the person you are there to see. If the woman's name is 'Carol Jones', there may be two 'Ms Jones', or two 'Carols' in the property and you could find yourself talking to the wrong one, which would be extremely unprofessional.
- When you are explaining who you are and who you work for, keep it very general.
- Once you know you are speaking to the person you have come to see, explain who you are and who you work for, but use words that make sense to anyone. If you name job titles and teams/departments that mean nothing to them, it can be irritating or intimidating. For example, if you say, 'I am a community family worker and I work for the children and families team in the Upper Street office', it probably means nothing to most people. Whereas if you say, 'I work in Family Support for Islington Council', it is clear who you work for and you can explain your role when you go in.
- If the person at the door is not the person you are there to see, keep it as simple as in 'My name is Joanna and I work for Islington Council.' Do not go into any detail of why you want to see the person. You should only be discussing their business with them.
- If the service user is called and comes to the door but the other person is still there, you should not go into detail without checking the service user is happy to have the discussion in front of someone else.
- When you have established you are speaking to the right person, always show them your identification.

EXAMPLES OF CONVERSATIONS ON THE DOORSTEP

Non-Hostile Single Parent: Arranged Visit

Door opens.

You: Hello. My name is Joanna and I am looking for Carol Jones.

Ms Jones: That's me.

You: Hello, Ms Jones. I am Joanna Nicolas and I am a social worker. I work for Islington Council. Here's my ID.

Ms Jones: What do you want?

You: Do you remember getting a letter from me, saying I would like to come and see you today at 11a.m.?

Ms Jones: I can't remember.

You: That's fine, but I wrote to you asking if I could come and see you today about your children, Mary and James. I need to talk to you and I wonder if we could go inside?

It is not always as straightforward as this and we will now consider other situations.

Planned Visit to Ms Jones

Male answers the door.

You: Hello, I am looking for Carol Jones, is she here?

Male: Who are you?

You: My name is Joanna. I am from the council. Is Carol Jones here?

Male: What do you want?

You: Sorry but it is Ms Jones I am here to see. Is she here?

Male: CAROL! . . . there's a lady here from the council. Wants to talk to you.
Carol then comes to the door and the man remains there.

You: Hello, Carol. My name is Joanna Nicolas and I work for the council.
I would like to have a chat with you but it is rather personal, so I wonder
if I could come in and we could talk somewhere privately?
(Do not mention that you have written to arrange the appointment in front
of the man. If it is an abusive relationship, she may not have told her
partner about the letter.)

Carol: Come in then, if you're going to.

VISITING A HOSTILE FAMILY

If you are visiting a home where you know the family does not like working
with professionals, you need to take a different approach. As discussed in
Chapter 5, if it is a block of flats, park around the corner and walk round the
side of the building. If you are visiting a house, keep yourself as inconspicuous
as possible until you are on the doorstep and listen to see if you can hear
voices before you knock on the door.

If you are visiting someone who lives in a block of flats, again walk around
the side to stop yourself being seen. Professionals often stand out in many of
the areas we visit, particularly if we arrive in a car. Ring someone else's bell
and ask if they could let you in because you have a letter for Number 6 (that
should be a random number you have seen, not the flat you are actually
visiting). In my experience, someone will always let you in and some blocks
have a tradesman bell which lets you in before a certain time, so it is worth
trying that bell first. Before you knock on the door of the flat you are visiting,
again listen at the door to see if you hear voices or activity. By doing this, if all
goes quiet when you knock on the door and the family refuses to open the door
you have evidence that someone is present in the flat.

Planned Visit to Possibly Hostile Family

You knock on the door, having heard noises coming from inside the home. The noises stop, all goes quiet and the door is not answered. After you have knocked again, if there is still no response, call through the letter box. (Do not put your face close to the letter box in case there is an aggressive dog.)

You: Hello, Carol. It's Joanna here, from the council. I need to talk to you but I don't want to talk out here. It would be helpful if you would let me in, so we can talk privately.

My experience is that at this point the family knows when it is beaten and generally someone comes to the door and lets me in.

If the door is answered by the woman you presume to be Carol Jones:

You: Thank you.
(Said with a big smile and then carry on as in the example above.)

If the door is answered by a male:

Male: What do you want?

You: I am from the council and I am here to see Carol Jones. Is she here?

Male: What business is it of yours?

You: I am here to see Carol Jones. I would be grateful if you would tell me whether she is here, or not.

Male: Carol! There is some woman here to see you. Get here now!

You then have to make a judgement as to whether you feel it is safe to go in the home. You should never enter a property if you feel it is unsafe to do so and it would be perfectly acceptable in the scenario above to say firmly, 'I have come here to speak to Carol but I am not going to come into your home because you seem angry. Is everything alright, Carol?' If the male apologises and you consider it safe to enter the property, that is a judgement for you to make on the day. If Carol says everything is fine but you feel threatened by the man, you could arrange for her to come into the office at a time that is convenient for you both. You would then leave.

Reminder Box: You are a Professional

It is really important that you remain calm and professional. Do not let yourself be bullied into explaining why you are there. Unless the man is the father of the children, and in this scenario he is not, he has no right to know anything. Keep reminding yourself you are a professional and there to do a job.

If you have had no response to calling through the letter box, you will have to leave, but it is important to put in your recording that you heard noises in the flat before you knocked and that it then went quiet. It all helps to build up evidence.

OTHER SITUATIONS YOU MAY BE FACED WITH

An Enthusiastic or Aggressive Dog

It is perfectly acceptable to ask a family to put their dog away before you enter, as long as the way you ask is considerate of the fact that it is their house and you are the uninvited guest. I would simply say, 'I am so sorry but would it be possible for you to put your dog in another room before I come in? I am rather wary of dogs.' In almost all cases the family will do this. In an extreme case they may say, 'It's our house and it's up to us where the dog is. Not you.' In that case you need to become more assertive and I would suggest this as a response, 'I am sorry but I do need to speak to you today but I am very wary of dogs and I won't be able to come in if you will not put the dog in another room just while I am here. Can I just be clear? Are you saying you are not prepared to do that?' Again, you have to feel it is safe to enter a home and if you are too busy worrying about a snarling or licking dog, you are not going to be able to concentrate on what matters. Most importantly that is the children.

If the family refuses to put the dog away, I would simply say, 'I am sorry but I am not going to come in if you are not willing to put your dog away. So I am going to leave now and my office will be in touch.'

An Unsuitably Dressed Service User

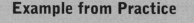

Example from Practice

On more than one occasion I have visited a home where the occupant was semi-naked when answering the door. On this occasion I was visiting a father, who knew I was due to visit. It was a hot summer's day and he answered the door dressed only in a small pair of Y fronts, which, I remember distinctly, had hearts on them. He invited me in and this was how the conversation went:

Him: Hello, Joanna. Do come in.

Me: Thank you, Jim, but I will wait here and give you some time to get dressed. (In other words, you are giving the impression that you thought he had forgotten your visit and was still getting dressed.)

Him: No. No. It's fine. It's so hot, I was in the garden. Come on through and we can sit outside.

Me: Thank you, Jim, but I would be grateful if you would get dressed first. As you know, I am here to talk about the children and it would be easier to do that if you were dressed. I'll just wait here until you are ready.

At which point Jim knew I was not going to go in until he was dressed, so, defeated, he got dressed and we had a constructive conversation about his children.

As in this example, it is very helpful, at times, to use closed statements but only when working with uncooperative families. We are always taught to use open questions 'How was your day?' as opposed to 'Did you have a good day?', 'How did you get that bruise?' not 'Did you get that bruise falling over?' However, if you are working with a family with whom you need to be assertive it can be much more effective to use closed statements at times, which leave little room for argument. This does not apply when you are undertaking the investigation, or assessing the level of risk but only in the context of making appointments, entering the home, seeing what you need to see in the home, etc. In Jim's case, my response to being invited to conduct the interview with Jim semi-naked was 'I will just wait here until you are ready.' If I had ended my part by saying 'Would that be OK?', it gives Jim room to manoeuvre.

Similarly, when you find yourself talking through a letter box, it is much more effective to say, 'Hello, Carol. It would be helpful if you would let me in, so we can talk privately' rather than 'Hello. Is anyone there?'

A Child Answers the Door

When the door is answered by a child, the first thing to do is to ask if Mummy/Daddy is there. What happens next will depend on the child's response and their age. If the child says 'Mummy's asleep' and it is a young child, I would ask them if they could be very clever and go and wake Mummy up, while I wait on the doorstep. If they come back and say they cannot wake her, you need to ensure that both mother and child are alright. If you feel it may be unsafe to enter the home, ring the police and stay there with the child until the police arrive. If you have no concerns for your personal safety, go into the home with the child, calling the mother's name loudly. If she in a bedroom, knock on the door loudly and call her name until she wakes up.

Example from Practice

I was visiting the home of two children, aged 18 months and 3 years. The mother was an alcoholic who was working with a voluntary organisation to try to stop drinking. She was a binge drinker and usually binged at weekends while her mother would care for the children.

It was a precarious situation and the children were subject to child protection plans. We were considering applying to the Court to remove the children because the mother refused to let her mother help more and she was becoming increasingly hostile towards those trying to help and support her.

I was doing an unannounced visit because I had my suspicions that the mother was doing a good job at covering up what was really happening and so when professionals did arranged visits, things were not too bad.

When I knocked on the door, the 3-year-old answered. I asked him if he could get Mummy but he said she was asleep. I said, 'Do you think you could be really clever and go and wake Mummy up?' He stood there, with his thumb in his mouth and shook his head. I realised that was not going to work, so I said, 'Are there any other grown-ups here?' (I wanted to know what I was walking into.) Again he shook his head, thumb not moving.

What to do?

I knew I could not leave. There were two small children unsupervised and a mother who may have been asleep, unconscious or even dead. I did not consider there to be a risk to myself if I went in alone, so it would have been a waste of police time to call them. I did not call my manager again because I was not concerned about my safety and I knew in this case I had to go into the home and find the mother, which I did. I went in slowly, calling her name all the time, while talking to the child. We went into the front room and there was the mother, asleep on the sofa with a large empty bottle of cider next to her and a mug of cider on the table. There were several empty bottles lying around and an ashtray full of cigarette ends, with a lighter and matches on the coffee table. The baby was sitting on the floor eating crisps.

I kept calling the mother's name until she woke up. She was still drunk and the first thing she did was tell me to p*** off. I ignored that and offered to make her a cup of tea, which she grudgingly agreed to. This gave her time to wake up without me being there and it also gave me a chance to see what state the kitchen was in and whether there was any food. The kitchen was in a terrible state and there was very little food. By the time I went back in the front room, the mother had composed herself a bit more but she was clearly drunk. I was not happy to leave the children alone with her. The baby was weighed down by her nappy and both the children were filthy. I was also concerned that the children had access to matches, a lighter and alcohol that looks like apple juice. I offered to change the baby's nappy, again it needed doing urgently and it gave me a chance to see the bedroom. There was no bedding in the cot, or on the 3-year-old's bed and an open plastic bag full of soiled nappies.

The mother agreed that she was having a bad day and that the children should go to her mother, until she felt better. I rang the grandmother and she came and took the children.

As always, you have to make a judgement. If there is no adult there, is the child old enough to be left alone? (There is no legal age that a child can be left alone; it depends entirely on the child and the circumstances.) Is it safe for you to enter the home? Should you call the police? Should you ring your manager for advice? Those are your options and you will have to make the decision based on the evidence you have. Figure 2.1 presents the possible choices to be made.

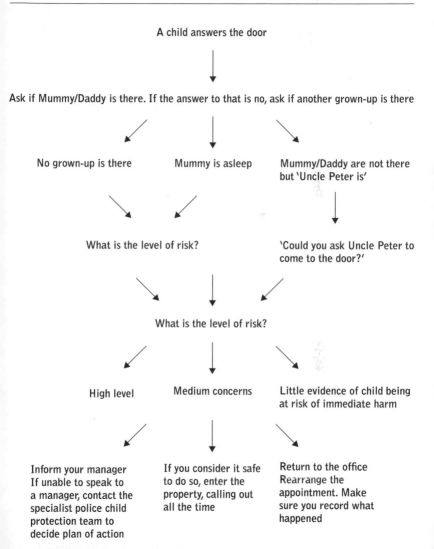

Figure 2.1 A child answers the door

The Person Answering the Door Does Not Speak English

Once you have established the person answering the door does not speak English, I would very clearly enunciate the name of the person you are there to see. You could also try writing it down and showing them the name. If you get nowhere with this, there is little you can do; you will most probably have to return with an interpreter.

If the person you are there to see comes to the door but they do not speak English, either you could try saying 'English?' and gesticulating into the home. In other words, is there anyone there who speaks English? If no one is forthcoming, you will have to return with an interpreter. If someone else comes forward who does speak English, first of all establish who they are and whether they are either any relation to the children, or the primary carer. If they are not, I would give away very little information. I would ask to see the children and then, depending on the circumstances, I would explain I will return with an interpreter. Try to agree a time with the primary carer then, as it will be difficult to communicate by telephone later.

As in all cases, your decision will depend on the urgency and purpose of your visit. Figure 2.2 presents the possible choices to be made.

If You Are Unable to Gain Entry

If you are unable to gain entry to a home for any reason, your first thought must be about the child you went to see. What is the level of risk to that child? Do you need to report straight back to your manager that you were unable to see the child? (This will depend on the level of risk.) For example, if you are doing the first home visit to a 3-day-old baby who is subject to a **child protection plan** following a **pre-birth child protection conference** and you are unable to see the baby, that must be taken very seriously. Always weigh up the risk to the child when considering your next course of action and always record when you have been unable to see the child. Figure 2.3 presents the possible choices to be made.

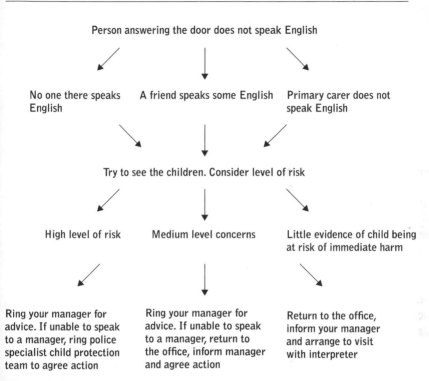

Figure 2.2 The person answering the door does not speak English

Good Practice Checklist for Getting in the Door

✓ Be assertive and don't go along with anything you feel uncomfortable about.
✓ Do not discuss details until you are sure you are talking to the right person.
✓ Used closed questions if necessary.
✓ Always assess the level of risk when making decisions.

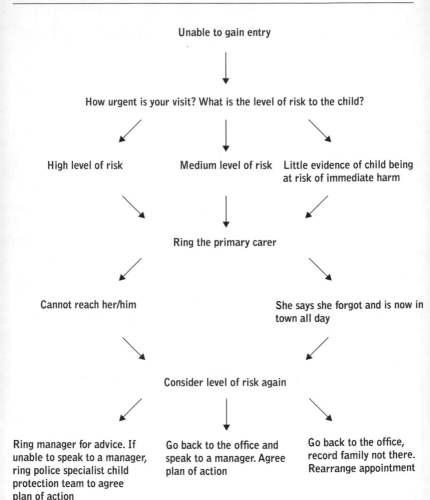

Figure 2.3 Unable to gain entry

3 Once in the Home

We have already established that in some high-profile child deaths professionals had missed some critical and key signs during the home visit. It is vital that we make best use of our time in the home and use all our skills to achieve a better understanding of what life is like for the child living there. This chapter will help to remind us what we are there to do and what our priorities should be.

SETTING UP THE INTERVIEW

The first thing is to establish who is in the room and who will remain for the interview. You are there to do a job. If the room is full of people, you must say to the person you are there to see that you need to talk to them but would not want to do so with so many others in the room.

Example from Practice

A social worker told me recently she was unable to have a satisfactory conversation with a mother during a child protection investigation because there were too many people in the room when she visited, all of whom were joining in. The visit was chaotic and the purpose of the visit – to ascertain the children's safety, in this case, was blurred by the many contributions.

If the room is full of people, you must explain, courteously but firmly to the person you have come to see that you need to talk to them privately. We cannot 'order' people to leave a room, nor can we insist we see a parent/carer alone but, as with all areas of our work, we have to make a judgement. If there are other people coming in and out of the room and expressing their opinions, it may well help us to judge the mood and atmosphere in the home but we will not gain the most from our conversation with the mother. And, as stated previously, we must be careful about disclosing confidential information in front of others.

✔ Good Practice Point: Identification

You have now got in to see 'Carol Jones' and are in her front room. There are also another older woman and two men in the room. You need to be mindful of the serious case review research that talks of 'shadowy men'. Ideally you should ascertain who these other adults are. You should certainly ask.

You: Thank you for agreeing to see me, Carol. Before we start talking, could I just ask who everyone is?

You: [Looking at 'man 1'] Hello, I am Joanna Nicolas. Could I ask who you are?

Man 1: I'm John.

You: Sorry, John who?

Man 1: John Evans.

You: Thank you, John.

(Repeat this with the other adults. Then say:)

You: As I said on the phone, I need to talk to you, Carol, but it is a personal matter and I would like to talk to you privately.

Carol: Anything you say to me, you can say in front of my mates.

You: I am afraid I can't because it is confidential. Is there another room we could go into, so we can talk privately?

(All this time you need to be pleasant but firm.)

Carol: I'm not moving.

Man 1: Neither am I.

You: Carol, you know I am here because I need to talk to you about the children. I am not going to do that in front of other people because it is confidential information. I need to talk to you privately. If you are telling me you are not prepared to do so, I will make a note of that, however, I would really like you to reconsider.

In this example Carol is being hostile and therefore I am being assertive. If I thought Carol was frightened of one or both of the men in the room, I would take a different approach – I would ask them questions first about their involvement with the children and with Carol and feel my way from there. Either way, we need to be asking who the men are. Men are too often over-looked in child protection work and we need to know who everyone around the child is.

So now you will have established who is in the room and who now remains in the room. You will be beginning to get an impression of what it might be like for the child living in this home and will become a vital part of your assessment.

GAINING ACCESS TO THE REST OF THE HOUSE

Just as we do not have right of entry to a property, we also do not have the right to look around the home without the parents' or carers' consent, but how can we do a thorough assessment of the child's situation if we have not seen where they sleep, eat and bathe? It is essential, when we are visiting a home as part of a child protection investigation, that we see the child's environment and if the family will not allow this, it should make us question why.

Example from Practice

Khyra Ishaq was a little girl who lived in Birmingham with her mother, her mother's partner and five siblings. She died in May 2008 and her mother and partner were convicted of her manslaughter. When she died, her weight was below the 0.4th centile and she was severely malnourished. Her siblings, who survived, were also severely malnourished. The family was known to health, education, social care and the police. Most professionals who attempted to visit the home were refused entry. In the words of the serious case review:

Living conditions within the household deteriorated over a period of months, it is now known that the mother wanted to be re-housed to larger premises, but was frustrated in this desire by the registered social landlord due to the state of decoration within the home, this in part due to the fact that the children had drawn pictures on the walls. At some point after the partner moved in to the household, the couple began a programme of refurbishment. It would appear, however, that this was not tackled in a systematic way and new projects were initiated, before the previous ones had been completed. This resulted in a constant reduction of habitable space within the house, eventually leading to only one upstairs bedroom, which all of the children occupied, a downstairs room which mother and partner shared and access to the kitchen, which was secured with a padlock and only accessible by the adults.[1]

If the police, who undertook a welfare visit, or the social workers who attempted to visit, had seen the inside of that house, they would have known that the situation was grave.

Reminder Box: Question Everything

If the family is preventing us from seeing the home, then that is very significant and needs to form part of our assessment.

This is not to suggest that as soon as you enter the home, you tell the parent or carer you need to see the entire house, that would be insensitive and poor practice, but if you are doing a child protection visit and you have not yet seen the bedrooms, kitchen, front room and bathroom, you need to do so, or record clearly why the parent is not willing to let you see the home.

While you are discussing this with the parent/carer, you must also be mindful of the fact that this is very intrusive. How would we like a complete stranger to go into our children's bedrooms? Again, this is a judgement call and it should depend on the level of concern. If the concern is that a young child is malnourished, unwashed, with dirty clothes, I would say you should be checking all of the house, as well as the cupboards and fridge for food.

Example from Practice

I was doing my first visit to a family where the mother was a known substance misuser; she was a single parent with two children under 3. Professionals had been involved since her first child was born and there were many concerns about neglect.

Two weeks prior to my visit, two Children's Centre workers had been in and cleaned her house from top to bottom, to show her what was expected of her. (Her home had always been very dirty, chaotic and dangerous for two young children.)

The day of my first visit as soon as I entered the home I could see it had deteriorated to its previous state. It was filthy and the baby was crawling around in dirt, old food, cat hair, etc. There was nowhere to sit in the sitting room because there were piles of clothes, papers and general clutter on every chair. There was also a low table with cigarette lighters, coffee cups, overflowing ashtrays, alcohol and drugs paraphernalia on it.

In the kitchen there was one packet of biscuits that the 2-year-old was helping himself to and some tea bags, that was it. There was nothing in the fridge, apart from some curdled milk.

Upstairs the children's bedroom smelt very strongly of urine and faeces. There was no bedding on the bed, or the cot, only grey mattresses, sodden with urine. There was a bare light bulb swinging from the ceiling, which was accessible from the bunk bed, which had a ladder propped up against it. The mother's bedroom was in an equally poor state and there were cat faeces on the floor. The bathroom and toilet were indescribably dirty and there was no toilet seat, or lid.

If I had only seen the first room I had been taken into, I would have had no idea about the state of the rest of the house. I could have made *an assumption* about the state of the rest of the house but that would be wrong I needed the evidence.

Only ask to see the rest of the house once you have had a conversation with the family and hopefully built up some kind of rapport with them. I am not suggesting any of this work is easy and it can be very difficult to ask someone if you can see their bedrooms, kitchen, bathroom, and then if you can look in their fridge and their cupboards; so here are some suggestions as to how you could phrase the questions:

Good Practice Point: See the Whole Picture

- Say: 'Carol, you know we are worried about the children. Part of what I am here to do is to see how things are at home, for you and the children. In order to do that I will need to see the rest of the house. If we could start with the children's bedrooms and work our way down.'
- Remember – never inform a family, when making an appointment to visit them, that you will need to see the whole house, as this then gives them the opportunity to change anything you may find that concerns you. Your assessment must include the child's bedroom.
- Say: 'Thank you for showing me the bedrooms, Carol. Now if I could just have a quick look at the bathroom.'
- Remember: do not overlook the bathroom, Victoria Climbié was kept in the bath and it is often the place where poor hygiene is evident.
- Say, when in the kitchen: 'Carol, you know that there are worries about the children's weight and what they are eating. I will need you to show me what is in the fridge and the cupboards, to show me what food you have in at the moment. I am sorry I have to ask you to do this but we need to make sure you have enough food and if you don't, we can help you with that.'
- Remember: your immediate concern should be whether the children have food that day or that week. The same would be true of baby milk and nappies. A longer-term concern would be whether the mother has an income and if she does, what she is spending her money on.

Point of Law: A Family Without Recourse to Public Funds[2]

We must never assume a family is in receipt of benefits if they are not working. Depending on the family's immigration status, they may not be entitled to public funds and this may impact on their ability to care for their children. It is our responsibility to make sure we understand the legal status of the families we are working with and what the possible impact on the children will be.

Reminder Box: Never Make Assumptions

Throughout this book I have warned against making assumptions. Do not assume that because the front room you have been shown into is immaculate, the rest of the house is too and do not assume that because you have seen one child's bedroom and have had no concerns, the others will be just the same. A particular child in a family can be scapegoated and treated very differently to the others.

Example from Practice

I was involved in an assessment of an uncle and aunt, who had recently had their niece and nephew placed with them in an emergency. They had no children of their own. The children had been living with their father but he took a drug overdose and was admitted to hospital. The children's mother was in prison. She was an intravenous drug user and she was in prison for stabbing the uncle, her brother, who was now caring for the children. The children were 8 and 4, a boy and a girl.

The uncle and aunt had shown great interest in the money they would receive if they were to care for the children, and there were some concerns about their motives. It was my job to assess and then recommend whether the children should remain with their aunt and uncle in the long term.

There were no concerns about the children's school attendance, appearance or appointment keeping. The home was immaculate and the children appeared to be well fed. The trouble was, I had a hunch that all was not as it seemed but I could not explain why. One day I asked the children to show me their rooms (this was not a child protection investigation but I knew it would give me greater insight into their lives and them, if I saw where they slept and played). First of all, the boy showed me his room, it was overflowing with cars, trains, Lego and books. There was plenty of furniture and it looked like a typical bedroom of a loved and wanted child. I was then taken by the little girl into her bedroom. In it there was a bed and a chair. That was it. There were no toys or books and no other furniture. When I asked her if she had any toys, very reluctantly, she went under her bed and brought out two pieces of Lego and a toy which had come free with a meal.

(Having worked in this field for a long time, there are not many situations that make me want to cry, but this was one of them. I dug my fingernails into my hands and admired the toys she had.)

What came to light was that the uncle hated the little girl because she looked like her mother. It was her mother who had stabbed the uncle, and in time he admitted that every time he looked at this little girl, she reminded him of the sister he hated and feared. Everything this little girl did was 'wrong', and that included spilling her drink, getting toothpaste on her clothes, wetting the bed. She was 4 years old and living in fear.

Needless to say, both those children were removed from the home.

TALKING TO THE CHILDREN

We keep seeing from serious case reviews that professionals do not talk to the children and sometimes do not even see them. There may be several reasons for this, the most common given by social workers is that there simply is not time to talk to children. I would suggest, however, that there may be some who are reticent to do so because they are unsure about how to set about it. If we do not feel confident about our ability to do something, we shy away from it, we feel uneasy and intimidated by it and so we avoid it. The trouble is that if we are nervous about talking to children, it rather loses the point of the work we are trying to do. How can we complete an assessment of a child if we do not talk to the child, observe the child and ask the child what they think? If you read/write in a report 'child seen', what does that actually mean? It is not enough to 'see' a child. We need to communicate with that child. This is a matter of enormous importance and concern, which should be addressed by the workforce.

Good Practice Box: Talking to the Child

■ Get down to the child's level, physically. Sit on the floor, or sit on the little chair.

- If you are in a young person's bedroom do not presume to sit on their bed. If there is nowhere else to sit, ask before you sit down and if they do not want you to, sit on the floor.
- Try to think of yourself as their equal. Do not patronise children or be condescending.
- Your interview technique must be relevant to the child's age. There is no point sitting down at a table with a 4-year-old and asking them lots of questions. You will achieve nothing. Play is a wonderful way to communicate with children: dolls, action figures, drawing, and if you think the family may not have toys to play with, take your own.
- Join in. Play with the child. Do your own drawing, make your own tower. If the child thinks you are engrossed in what you are doing, they will be more relaxed and may feel more able to talk. Keep on doing your drawing if a 5-year-old tells you, 'Daddy put his winkie in my bottom and it was sore.' If you stop and look at the child, they may well sense this is important and clam up. Remember, with an older child who knows they are telling you about abuse, you would take a different approach.
- The car can be the perfect place to talk. Many a time I have taken a circuitous route to our destination – I would never get a job as a cab driver. It is often easier to talk if we are not being looked at in the eye and a car often feels a safe place to talk for a child.
- Depending on the child's age, explain why you are there and what the likely outcome is. Children often report that we ask them lots of questions but tell them nothing. They will want to know and deserve to know, what is going on.
- You need to be sure you understand what the child is telling you and you are not making assumptions. For example, I knew a small boy, who at the age of 2–3 loved playing with sticks and wherever we were, he would find a stick. The only problem was he could not say 'stick' but instead would say 'dick'. He was always telling anyone who would listen how he loved playing with dicks. It would have been easy to jump to the wrong conclusion. Equally another little girl is currently obsessed with binoculars, however, she calls them 'knockers' and is always asking her mother for her 'knockers'. Beware of making assumptions.

The other point to make about language is that it moves on and again we can make assumptions about what a young person is saying to us. (I remember telling my nephew about a present I had bought for someone and he kept saying it was 'sick'. I was rather offended and surprised because normally he is very polite and lovely. It was only later on in the conversation I realised that 'sick' meant 'cool'!)

When we are visiting a family at home, we cannot insist we see the child alone and of course it will depend on their age and ability. It is difficult to generalise but if I am meeting a child for the first time and they are under 2, I would not presume to see them alone. With a child of 3, or 4, I may well say to the mother that I need to see the child's bedroom and I would really like to speak to the child. I would then ask the child to show me their bedroom. I would only do that when I had been in the home for a little while and had probably been sitting on the floor, playing with a toy with the child while I spoke to the mother.

SEEING A SLEEPING BABY

If we are told, when we visit a home that the baby is asleep, and we cannot see them, we need to weigh up the risks. This book is about home visits in child protection cases and I would argue that we cannot come away from a home without seeing the baby. It is the under-1s who are the most vulnerable and if we are assessing the level of risk, we need to see the baby. We need to explain that to the primary carer and it may be that you are satisfied by standing at the bedroom door and seeing the baby is asleep and breathing.

Reminder Box: Waking the Baby

Only wake a baby in extreme circumstances, unless it is your job to weigh the baby, or examine the baby, as part of the child protection work.

As always, the actions we take are based on our own professional judgement but if in doubt, we should seek advice from others who have more experience. Remember, we are all learning all the time.

Good Practice Checklist: Once in the Home

✓ Establish who is in the home at the time of your visit, and ask for names and relationship to the children.
✓ Ensure that you see the entire house, particularly the children's bedrooms.
✓ Talk to the children using techniques relevant to their age.
✓ Ensure that you see sleeping babies.

What to look out for
Using observational skills

CLUES AND IMPRESSIONS FROM THE CHILD

As professionals, we need to know about child development. There can only be general rules and there will always be exceptions but part of our assessment of the child should be how they present physically and emotionally. A young child may well be wary of a stranger and that is a natural response. Most young children look to their primary carer for reassurance, either with a look or by moving closer, while in contrast a child who is neglected may well be much more forward. How often do we experience a 3-year-old who, on our first visit to the family, climbs on our knee and tries to claim our attention – perhaps thrusting a book in our face? It may well be that the child is so desperate for attention, that he has lost his natural caution but it may not be; so again do not make an assumption. What other evidence is there that would support the theory that this child is starved of attention?

Example from Practice

I was working with a woman who had recently fled from an abusive relationship. She was living with her five children aged between 8 months and 12 years. One day I was visiting the family, the baby was in his usual position lying in a pushchair with a bottle. I was at the property for an hour and a quarter, and during my visit children returned from school, uniformed police visited, there were several arguments and lots of tears. Throughout all the commotion, the baby fed himself, fell asleep, dropped the bottle, woke up, found the bottle, fed himself, dropped the bottle, could not find it again and lay there staring at the wall. During that whole time the baby asked nothing of anyone and did not make a noise. He had learnt early on that there was no point crying because no one responded. He was also unable to sit unsupported, in this case evidence that because he spent most of his time strapped in a pushchair, his muscles were not developing as they should.

> Remember that if there are concerns about a child's development, there should always be a clinical assessment by a medic.

DISGUISED COMPLIANCE

This is a term first used by Peter Reder, Sylvia Duncan and Moira Gray (1993). The NSPCC defines the term as meaning as 'A parent or carer giving the appearance of co-operating with child welfare agencies to avoid raising suspicions, to allay professional concerns and ultimately to diffuse professional intervention.' We saw this with Peter Connelly's mother, Tracey Connelly. She presented as a mother who was concerned about her son, who took him to the doctor when he had injuries from 'falls'. It is easy to be lulled into a false sense of security by the parent/carer who ostensibly is caring and doing all that is asked of them. We need to look beyond – what is the evidence that the child's life is improving? (In Peter Connelly's case, his weight plummeted from being on the 75th centile when he was born, to the 9th centile at the time of his death.)

A recent serious case review, SCRCE00 East Cheshire, in February 2011,[1] concluded that the approach of 'many professionals' was affected by perceptions and assumptions made regarding the parents' social class, professional status, and high academic qualifications.

[Professionals were] lulled by the parents' disguised compliance. They presented as being concerned for Child B's welfare – which to an extent they may have been. They usually reported him missing, and often made efforts themselves to locate him. In addition they were active in supporting the school's efforts to deal with his challenging behaviour and running away from school.

We need to be clear that part of our assessment will be what we are told by those around the children but greater weight should be given to the evidence. Is the situation improving for the child?

As always, we need to be open and honest with the families we are working with – tell a parent if you believe they are trying to deceive or manipulate you, and explain your reasons. Do not be confrontational but present them with the evidence.

For example, 'I know you have made it very clear that you support the therapeutic work that the Child and Adolescent Mental Health Service is doing with your child but actually X has missed four appointments because you have said you have been unable to get him there and you have not attended the two appointments you have been offered. I would like to talk about why that is.'

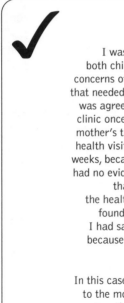

Good Practice Point: Sharing Information

I was working with a mother who had two children, and both children were subject to child protection plans because of concerns of neglect. One of the children had a serious skin condition that needed careful and constant management. As part of the plan, it was agreed the mother would take the child to the health visitor's clinic once a week, so she could monitor the skin condition and the mother's treatment of it. After a few weeks the mother told me the health visitor had said she only needed to go to the clinic every two weeks, because she was managing the skin condition well. Although I had no evidence at that point, my gut instinct about this mother was that she was devious and manipulative. I contacted the health visitor to verify what the mother had told me. I then found out that the mother had told the health visitor that I had said she only needed to go to the clinic every two weeks because I was no longer concerned about her treatment of the skin condition.

In this case, the health visitor and I agreed we would do a joint visit to the mother. She needed to know that we were working closely together (this is even more important in cases of disguised compliance). We had a discussion with the mother and she came away knowing that with this issue she could not pull the wool over our eyes. She continued to be a challenge to work with.

> ✓ **Good Practice Box: Holding Babies**
>
> As part of observing how children present physically and emotionally, we should be holding babies. It is not suggested that as soon as you go into a home, you ask to hold the baby but when you have been there a while, talking to the **primary carer**, while making eye contact with and cooing at the baby, ask the primary carer if you can hold him/her. We can learn a lot from how responsive a baby is, whether the baby looks to his/her primary carer for reassurance, whether the primary carer hands the baby over without a care. You may also be able to tell if the baby has any physical injuries when you hold him/her – there may be a limb that hangs awkwardly, the baby may cry out when you move him/her.

OBSERVING HOW THE CHILD PLAYS

In Chapter 3 we looked at how to communicate with children. In this chapter we are looking at what to observe. While we are talking to others in the home, we should observe the child. Are they playing?, is there anything to play with?, how are they playing? There is so much to learn from observing the child in their home environment.

> **Example from Practice**
>
> During a home visit I was in deep conversation with the mother. Her 8-year-old son was playing on the floor. He was playing with a child's doctor's kit and I noticed the child pick up the plastic syringe and 'inject' himself in his arm, having bent his elbow. His mother was an intravenous drug-user. He knew exactly what to do with a syringe.

OBSERVING HOW THE ADULTS AND CHILDREN INTERACT

There is a considerable amount of research that tells us of the importance of a child having a primary carer who is able to prioritise their child's needs above their own. This now forms the basis of attachment theory, which was first defined by John Bowlby in the 1940s and went on to be developed by Mary Ainsworth, in particular and many others (Bowlby 1951; Ainsworth 1968; Ainsworth et al. 1974). As part of our assessment, it is essential we ascertain whether the child we are working with has this positive attachment.

✓ **Good Practice: Observing the Adults and Children Together**

- Watch how the adults in the home respond to the child – do they respond?
- Does the primary carer respond to the baby's cry, or is he/she so absorbed in telling you his/her own problems?
- Does the primary carer just put the dummy back in the baby's mouth, without making eye contact and continue talking about him/herself?
- Does the primary carer stop to pick up the baby and soothe him/her?
- Does the baby demand anything of the primary carer?
- Does the child look to the mother for reassurance (this is a natural response in a young child) or does the child come straight to you and ignore the mother?
- Does the primary carer answer all the questions you put to the child?
- Does the child appear fearful, or watchful?
- Is the primary carer controlling the interview?
- Does the child flinch when the primary carer moves quickly?
- How would you describe the atmosphere in the room?

Example from Practice

I was visiting the home of a family where there were concerns about physical abuse of the children. The father was present and during the meeting he walked quickly to where his 3-year-old son was sitting on the floor. The father was not angry but as he approached his son, the boy cowered and covered his head with his arms. That action gave a very clear picture of what that child's experience with his father was.

We can also learn a lot from how a child responds to their primary carer becoming upset, or angry. Does the child register emotion, or do they appear to be oblivious to the tears, the raised voice? I heard of a mother recently who became very upset and her 3-year-old son said to her, 'Have your pills, Mummy, and you will feel better.' In his world, that was what you did, if you were sad.

Reminder Box: Cultural Differences

Child protection is an area where we need to pay particular heed to cultural differences. It is easy to make an assumption that the Black, African mother who does not play with her child does not have a positive attachment to her child. We need to find out more. Maybe she comes from a tribe where the children play together and the mothers do not have time to play because they have to collect the water, find the firewood, cook the food and wash the clothes in the river, among other things. Even understanding that, it may remain a concern because that mother is no longer living with her tribe but lives in isolation in a tower block and the child has no input from anyone.

However, if we understand why there is so little communication between the mother and the child, at least we can think about what support we can offer that mother, in the alien environment she is living in.

OBSERVING HOW THE ADULTS IN THE HOME PRESENT

There are many factors that affect how children are treated by their families. As stated previously, there is a strong link between parents and carers being perpetrators or victims of domestic abuse, suffering from mental ill-health and/or abusing substances and the children in those families being abused and/or neglected. The risk to the child increases exponentially if more than one of those factors is in place.

Reminder Box: Parent with Mental Illness

It is important to stress that just because a parent has a diagnosed, or undiagnosed, mental illness, does not automatically mean that their child will be being abused and/or neglected. It depends entirely on what the illness is and whether the parent/carer is willing or able to accept they have an illness.

Here are two contrasting examples.

Example from Practice 1

A mother I worked with had been diagnosed as suffering from bi-polar disorder. She had a very good understanding of her illness and was willing to accept she had a mental illness. She shared the care of her children with her mother because she could not manage all the time on her own but she was a devoted mother. She would say to the professionals, 'You will know when I am going downhill because I will stop wearing make-up and I will smell'. She usually wore a lot of make-up and personal hygiene was not an issue. Sure enough, I would visit one day and she would look a bit rough. I would visit the next day and she would look terrible. I would then contact her community psychiatric nurse. She had periods where she was very unwell and had to be hospitalised. During those times the arrangement she had made with her mother was that her mother would care for the children full-time. On her return home she always needed some time to paint the flat – during her manic phases she would paint the flat in psychedelic colours – and once she had restored order, she was as capable and as loving as any other mother, always putting her children's needs before her own.

Example from Practice 2

I worked with another mother who was completely unable or unwilling to accept that she suffered from mental ill-health. Her illness rendered her incapable of caring for her children. She had periods where she would not sleep for several days at a time but would remain awake and talk constantly, regardless of whether anyone was in the room. She would become paranoid about ghosts and aliens taking over her home and forget she had children. Sometimes she saw her children as the threat. The Court removed her children because she was unable to care for them. Perhaps if she had been willing to have a mental health assessment, her illness might have been treated and she might have been able to care for her children. Sadly, we will never know.

It is vital that we guard against feeling so much compassion for the adult victim of domestic abuse, the mother who is an intravenous drug user, who was sexually abused as a child, the mother who is a victim of domestic abuse and now abuses alcohol to blot out the terror of her daily life, that we forget why we are there. We are there because there are concerns a child is being neglected and/or abused and it is the child who must remain the focus of our visit and the focus of our work and our assessments.

Good Practice Point: Observing How the Animals in the Home Present

There are strong links between the abuse of animals and the abuse of women and children. If there is an emaciated dog, that snarls and shakes, we need to think why that might be and ask questions.

OBSERVING THE STATE OF THE HOME

We have already considered this question in terms of general conditions in Chapter 3. What I want you to do now is consider it in the context of any issues there may be in the home. I have been in more homes than I can number where there have been punch holes in the doors and dents in the walls and yet the family assures me there are no issues of violence – do we all have punch marks in our walls?

Good Practice Point: Maintain Your Position in Court

✔

I was involved in a court case where the father wanted unsupervised contact with his newborn baby. He had been assessed by an 'expert' whose conclusion was that this man was no longer using cannabis habitually and no longer drank alcohol to excess – this conclusion was based on self-reporting by the father. In court, his barrister argued that as he did not have 'issues with his anger' he should be allowed unsupervised contact with his baby. (He was not living with the mother of the baby.) When I was cross-examined by his barrister, I told the court that I disagreed with the conclusion. There really was an audible gasp in the courtroom that I, a lowly social worker, had dared to disagree with an eminent psychologist, who was an expert. What the psychologist had not done but I had was spend time in this man's home, with his mother, with whom he lived. I had seen the punch marks in the doors. I had seen the doors broken off their hinges and I had heard her fear about his anger. He did not deny to me that he spent most of each day and night in his bedroom, playing violent computer games and smoking cannabis and had done so for many years. He had no job and no friends, his world was his room and when he ventured out, his mother was fearful of his rages.

I had the evidence because of those home visits. The psychologist had his word.

The court did not allow him unsupervised contact and contact was not allowed to take place at his home, which was what he had wanted, but at a Children's Centre.

Everything in this chapter emphasises the importance of our observational skills and using those to back up the evidence we have. In Chapter 2, I warned of assuming the chaotic household will have neglected children in it. The most important factor of a child's life is to have one person who gives unconditionally of themselves. It might be that their mother cannot keep on top of the washing, the washing up, the cleaning, but if she loves her child, can put her child's needs before her own and meet her child's needs, that is what counts the most. In an ideal world we, as parents, would do it all. Sometimes that is not possible. It is up to us as professionals to remember what is important and what really matters to that child. Just as a primary carer must prioritise their child, so must we as professionals be clear about and prioritise what matters most.

Good Practice Checklist: Using Your Observational Skills

✓ Beware of 'disguised compliance' – never assume that what you are being told by a parent or carer is the truth.

✓ Always hold babies to assess their relationship with the primary carer.

✓ Observe how the adults and children respond to each other.

✓ Observe how the child plays.

✓ Look out for anything unusual in the physical appearance of the home, e.g. punch holes in walls.

Keeping yourself safe

This chapter will give you some practical tips to keep yourself safe when home-visiting, based on my experiences and others around me, over the past 17 years. Experts in this field, such as Ray Braithwaite, have written a lot on this topic, so please refer to the Further Reading and Resources section if you wish to expand your knowledge base.

As any child protection social worker will tell you, we are often in situations where adults and sometimes children are hostile and aggressive. I have never been physically assaulted but I have had my life threatened and been verbally abused and sworn at on many occasions.

We never know when a situation may turn nasty and so we always need to be aware of that when we are going into people's homes and discussing a very sensitive subject. We know that many of the parents we work with will be perpetrators or victims of domestic abuse, many will be misusing substances and many will suffer mental ill-health. None of those factors lead automatically to violence, but may well exacerbate an already delicate situation.

As I have said throughout this book, we need to be prepared. Forewarned is forearmed. The more we know about the people who live in the home, the better prepared we will be.

It is not just our responsibility to keep ourselves safe. Our employers have responsibilities too. There is also health and safety legislation. If you feel it is putting your safety at risk to visit a particular home alone, or even with another worker, you need to make that clear to your manager. There is an element of risk in the work we do and that is unavoidable. In the words of Professor Munro (2011), we need to be 'risk aware, not risk averse'. Professor Munro is actually talking about the risks we have to take in child protection work but it is just as true for us when we are visiting people's homes.

It is clearly not realistic to keep saying you do not want to go into this home or that home but if there is a genuine case for not visiting a home, either alone or with another professional, you must state your case. It can be very hard to stand your ground; the team is busy, there is too much to do and you are 'making things difficult' by saying you want someone to go with you. A good manager will accept that and support you. However, you may not always have a good manager. Do not allow yourself to be railroaded if you are genuinely concerned.

Reminder Box: One Rule for the Child, One for You?

You should also ask yourself why it is OK for a child to be living in the home when you and other professionals are too afraid for your personal safety to visit it. You should raise this with your manager.

Example from Practice

I was working with a family where the children were living with an uncle who was known to be extremely violent. He had spent many years in prison and was well known to the police. He was a perpetrator of domestic abuse, he had assaulted many individuals including police officers and he self-harmed, often deliberately cutting himself in stressful situations with professionals. He was also an alcoholic.

On his release from his latest prison sentence it fell upon me to tell him we had a court order in place. The court had decided he was only to have supervised contact with his nephews and nieces that he had brought up.

I was not prepared to see this man alone, or somewhere where my safety could not be guaranteed. It was agreed that two of us would see him in a room with two exits and we took everything out of the room except the chairs we were sitting on – we knew he had a propensity to throw things at people when under pressure. We also had four police officers, hidden nearby. (He did not like police officers and often reacted violently towards them and therefore they needed to remain hidden.)

As is so often in these situations, by the time he arrived my heart was racing and I expected a huge, furious man to come bursting in, swearing and throwing punches. The reverse was true. It was the first time I had met 'Pete' and when I went into reception to collect him, there stood a small, dejected man. Meeting Pete that day reminded me that many of our perpetrators are victims too. He had grown up in a brutal house, his parents were both alcoholics, there was domestic abuse and he was a victim of physical abuse and neglect.

The meeting passed without incident but then it came to who was going to supervise his contact with his children. In the team I worked in at the time it was the role of a family support worker to supervise contact, however, in this case we agreed that would not be safe. My manager wanted me to do it but I was not prepared to because of my personal safety. I am a mother and my priority was to keep myself safe for my children. That is not to say that only parents should have regard to their personal safety or greater priority but in my case my children come first and I was adamant I would not do it. I felt very guilty about my decision – I was depriving the children from seeing their uncle, I was making things difficult for my team manager but I stood my ground.

In the end the team manager supervised the contact sessions, which is highly unusual and they passed without incident until Pete stopped coming.

There are many definitions of violence. The Health and Safety Executive defines violence as 'Any incident, in which an employee is abused, threatened or assaulted by a member of the public in circumstances arising out of the course of employment.'[1] Surveys of social workers tell us that verbal abuse and threats of violence are common, as they are with some health professionals and others. It is a delicate balance. Abuse comes with the territory, but that is not to excuse abuse or to allow it to continue, but we have to accept is as part of our job and learn how best to deal with it.

KEEPING YOURSELF AS SAFE AS POSSIBLE: BE PREPARED

■ Find out everything you can about who lives in the home. If you have good connections with your local housing department that can often be a good way to check if there have been any reported incidents of anti-social behaviour at that address. You will not need to do this for every single home you visit but it can enhance information you already have if there are already some concerns.

■ In all cases you should make sure your team has a good system for checking in, and if there is not one in place, make it happen. Do not forget, your employer has responsibilities too. Many teams have large boards where staff write where they are and when they are due to return. If your writing is illegible, like mine, make sure you write clearly. (I used to have a team manager who would write R.I.P at least once a month in her slot, when she was out of the office. It always looked rather gloomy but actually it stood for 'Research in practice' and these were monthly meetings she would attend.) Be clear about where you are going and who you are seeing.

■ Again, many teams have a 'buddy' system, someone you always check in with, to ensure you are safely back. Be proactive, be the one to set systems up, if they are not already in place.

■ Make sure your mobile is charged. If you are visiting somewhere that does not have mobile reception, there may be a greater argument for doing a joint visit, if you are concerned about your safety.

■ If you are visiting somewhere you are not sure is safe, try to do it in daylight hours in the winter.

■ If you are visiting a big estate where there are lots of tower blocks, it can be quite intimidating. Try to find out exactly where you are going before the visit, rather than wandering round looking lost.

■ If you know there is domestic abuse, it may be helpful to find out when the perpetrator is not there, in the first instance. It will be more likely you could have an honest and open conversation if the controlling partner is not there.

■ Think about how you present yourself. Apart from the professional aspect, if you needed to, could you run in the clothes and shoes you have chosen to wear?

Reminder Box: Don't Ignore the Father

If the perpetrator of the domestic abuse is the father, we must not ignore fathers; research from serious case reviews [2] tells us that fathers are often overlooked. Even if the father is the perpetrator of domestic abuse, only visiting in his absence may keep us safe but means our risk assessment for the children we are there to protect will be incomplete.

JOINT VISITS

As stated in previous chapters, there can be many reasons why we do a joint visit with another professional. This chapter is only considering a joint visit from a safety point of view.

The key point is, we are less physically vulnerable if there are two of us and most people are less likely to be intimidating/threatening/violent if there is a witness. However, there are always exceptions to every rule. Two colleagues of mine were assaulted by a service user when they visited her home together.

Make sure you have a plan. Discuss what you will do if the service user becomes aggressive. It may be helpful for you, the social worker, to deal with the issues that bring you there – leaving your colleague to deal with any hostile behaviour.

Consider where you park your car. If you are visiting a large estate, people may have learnt who you are and what car you drive. Park somewhere so that your car can be seen from the window – one of you can then keep an eye on the car, while the other, probably you as the social worker, goes about the visit.

ONCE IN THE HOME

Think about where you are in someone's home. Make sure you sit near the door, so you can leave – quickly if you have to. A good tip is to let the service user lead the way into the room, so that they will take the chair furthest away from the door. You can then sit in the chair nearer the door. Social workers (and I am sure other professionals) have been known to climb out of windows. It is easier to use the door.

Be mindful of any items around you that could be used as potential weapons. You cannot guard against everything but I do remember asking a service user if he would mind removing the samurai sword that was sitting on the kitchen table.

Make sure you have an exit strategy if the situation becomes too dangerous. There are many different ways of doing this. I would suggest you are honest and straightforward, and address any threatening behaviour straight away. Keep it very simple and say something like 'I can see you are extremely angry and we cannot carry on with this meeting while you are so cross. I am also not prepared to be shouted at. I am going to leave now and I will telephone you later, when you have had a chance to calm down and we can then discuss what is going to happen next.'

Reminder Box: Be Assertive

Remind yourself you are there to do a job but there is absolutely no reason why you should allow yourself to be threatened or shouted at.

Example from Practice

I went to see a mother to talk about her 13-year-old daughter, who was making herself vulnerable by associating with older men who were considered to be a risk to children. The mother appeared to have little interest in her daughter's whereabouts and wanted to talk about her housing problems. Each time I turned the conversation back to her daughter, she became more irate until finally she leapt up, came over to me and leaned over me and shouted at me that she was going to hit me, unless I listened to her problems. She also swore at me. I stood

> up slowly and moved away from her towards the door, calmly telling her I
> was not going to listen to her if she was going to be abusive. I was going to leave
> and we would be in touch. (It was only when I was safely in my car that I started
> shaking like a leaf. It is very frightening being verbally abused and physically
> threatened.)

LANGUAGE

We have to take some of the responsibility for what happens during a home visit. Professionals can be quick to blame the family but we also have a part to play. The language we use is so important. I have already warned against using jargon. If your defence mechanism is to use jargon, and you become increasingly defensive, you may use language the service-user does not understand and that will only inflame the situation.

You must not allow yourself to become angry when confronted with an angry service user. If you become angry too, it will only inflame the situation. Try to remain calm and assertive.

As Ray Braithwaite says, 'Leaving is always an option. Leave by deception ("I'll just need to get my diary from the car"); walking away positively; making a statement to assist ("Let's take a break") or even running if necessary.'

FOLLOW-ON ACTIONS

All threats should be taken seriously and reported to your manager. Your organisation's procedures should be followed to ensure the correct response, according to the level of threat, is taken.

Remember too that just as it is OK to say you do not know something, it is also OK to say you were scared. It is your organisation's responsibility to ensure you are safe at work, but as well as that, I believe the best sort of de-briefing is often done with our team members. Strong, supportive teams produce happy, healthy workers. We always hear about the sick sense of humour of those working in crisis situations. Humour can be a wonderful coping mechanism for reducing distress created by stressful situations. You are not a better person for internalising the stress of your job. You are not weak if you say you are frightened. There is so much said about workers becoming 'burnt out'. I believe that if we look after ourselves and look after each other, there is much less chance of that happening.

Reminder Box: Be Alert

Be prepared, be alert and report any concerns. That is your best chance of avoiding situations that become dangerous.

Good Practice Checklist: What to Do to Keep Yourself Safe

✓ Make the appointment during daylight hours in the winter, if possible.
✓ Let the office know where you are going and when you will be back.
✓ Let your 'buddy' know.
✓ Take your charged mobile and pre-programme in 999 and your office number.
✓ Let people know when you have left the home, so they know you are safe.

Glossary

The glossary will not only explain terms used in the book, it will also cover some of the common denominators there are in child protection and the impact of those denominators on our visits to families. Glossary words are given in bold on their first occurrence in the text.

The glossary will also explain terminology.

TERMINOLOGY

What is the difference between 'safeguarding children' and 'child protection'?

Many professionals use the words interchangeably, as if they mean the same thing. They don't. According to the Children's Workforce Development Council:

> Safeguarding means proactively seeking to involve the whole community in keeping children safe and promoting their welfare. Child protection is a central part of safeguarding and promoting welfare. It is the process of protecting individual children identified as either suffering or at risk of suffering significant harm as a result of abuse or neglect.

What does 'child protection' mean?

The Children Act, 1989, introduced the concept of significant harm as the threshold which justifies compulsory intervention in family life in the best interest of children. The Local Authority has a statutory duty to make enquiries where it has reasonable cause to suspect a child is suffering, or is likely to suffer significant harm (Section 47).

DEFINITIONS

Care Order s.31, Children Act, 1989: These orders are usually sought by a Local Authority (although the NSPCC can bring proceedings, it is extremely rare for them to do so) in respect of children whom they believe are suffering or are likely to suffer significant harm. A care order will last until the child is 18, unless discharged earlier. The Local Authority will have parental responsibility, alongside the parents with parental responsibility, for the child subject to a care order.

Child protection plan:

We used to talk about children on the 'At Risk Register' or 'the Child Protection Register', we now talk about children who are subject to or on a 'child protection plan'. In order for a child to be subject to a child protection plan, there will have been a child protection conference. It will have been decided by the professionals at the conference that the child should be made the subject of a child protection plan and the categories of abuse will have been agreed. The conference will meet again, initially after three months, and then every six months, to decide whether the child needs to remain subject to a plan and whether anything else needs to be considered. In the meantime the key professionals and family members, known as the core group, will be meeting regularly to make sure the plan is effective in keeping the child safe and everyone is doing as they should. It is important to remember it is how the professionals work together and how the family works with the professionals that keep the child safe, not 'the plan'.

When there is a child protection plan in place, it is where there is a high level of concern but the child is still thought to be safe in the home. (Some Local Authorities place children on *interim care orders* at home but this is not common.)

Child protection conference:

Professionals will decide that there needs to be a child protection conference. A child protection conference brings together all the professionals working with the family and the family itself. Reports by the professionals will be submitted to the conference and then those attending the conference will give their professional views, as to what the concerns and positives are. If the decision of the professionals at the conference is that the child should be made subject to a *child protection plan*, they will then have to agree which categories of abuse the child is at risk of. The child protection plan will be drawn up with the family and worked on by the *core group*, who will have been identified at the conference.

Common themes in child protection work:

For many years the UK government has analysed the data that has come from serious case reviews and the research is then published. This research enables us to see common themes, three of which are most prevalent and therefore significant.

Although we must always keep our focus on the child, that does not mean we should see a child in isolation. We must consider what life is like for that child and what their perception of their world is. It is the adults around the child who will have the greatest impact on the child, from the time it is born, until it moves out into the wider world. What the research shows us is that in a significant number of cases, there are substance misuse, mental ill-health or domestic abuse issues with the adults with whom the abused/neglected child is living and that the risk to the child increases exponentially if more than one of these factors is involved.

Before we visit a family, we should have as much information as possible about that family and any factors that are relevant, first and foremost to the child but also to us, when we visit. For example, if you are visiting a family and you know the mother has a diagnosis of bi-polar disorder, you need to understand what that means and how that may impact on your visit.

Core group:

When it is decided at a child protection conference that the child needs to be made subject to a *child protection plan*, the core group will be identified by the conference. It will consist of the key professionals involved with the family and the key family members. The core group will work on the child protection plan and will meet ten days after the initial *child protection conference* and then monthly until the next conference. It is their responsibility to monitor and implement the child protection plan and ensure the child remains safe within the home.

Emergency Protection Order, s.44 Children Act, 1989:

The Local Authority can apply to the Court for an emergency protection order. That gives the Local Authority the power to remove the children from the family. The Order lasts for eight days and can be extended for a further seven.

Emotional abuse:

"Emotional abuse is the persistent emotional maltreatment of a child such as to cause severe and persistent adverse effects on the child's emotional development.

It may involve conveying to children that they are worthless or unloved, inadequate, or valued only insofar as they meet the needs of another person. It may include not giving the child opportunities to express their views, deliberately silencing them or 'making fun' of what they say or how they communicate.

It may feature developmentally inappropriate expectations being imposed on children. These may include interactions that are beyond the child's developmental capability, as well as overprotection and limitation of exploration and learning, or preventing the child participating in normal social interaction.

It may involve seeing or hearing the ill treatment of another. It may involve serious bullying (including cyber bullying), causing children frequently to feel frightened or in danger, or the exploitation or corruption of children.

Some level of emotional abuse is involved in all types of maltreatment of a child, though it may occur on its own."
Working Together to Safeguard Children, 2010.

Interim Care Order, s.38 Children Act, 1989:

An interim care order lasts for eight weeks, initially. It may be granted to a Local Authority when they apply for a care order for a child, while assessments are carried out and long-term plans for the child decided. When there is an interim care order in place, the Local Authority has shared parental responsibility for the child named in the order.

Neglect:

"Neglect is the persistent failure to meet a child's basic physical and/or psychological needs, likely to result in the serious impairment of the child's health or development. Neglect may occur during pregnancy as a result of maternal substance abuse. Once a child is born, neglect may involve a parent or carer failing to do the following:

- Provide adequate food, clothing and shelter (including exclusion from home or abandonment).
- Protect a child from physical and emotional harm or danger.
- Ensure adequate supervision (including the use of inadequate care-givers).
- Ensure access to appropriate medical care or treatment.
- Neglect of, or unresponsiveness to, a child's basic emotional needs."

Working Together to Safeguard Children, 2010.

Parental responsibility:

Parental responsibility is defined by the Children Act, 1989, as 'all the rights, duties, powers, responsibilities and authority which by law a parent of a child has in relation to the child and his property'. Therefore, if you have parental responsibility, you have all the legal powers to make appropriate decisions in relation to the upbringing of your child. When there is an emergency protection order, *interim care order* or care order in place, the Local Authority 'shares' parental responsibility with the parents. I put the word 'share' in inverted commas because I believe it is an unhelpful euphemism. The Local Authority has greater power than the parents, if any of the above orders are in place.

As a parent with parental responsibility, you will never lose parental responsibility unless your child is adopted.

Physical abuse:

"Physical abuse may involve hitting, shaking, throwing, poisoning, burning or scalding, drowning, suffocating, or otherwise causing physical harm to a child. Physical harm may also be caused when a parent or carer fabricates the symptoms of, or deliberately induces, illness in a child." Working Together to Safeguard Children, 2010. It now constitutes physical abuse if a child is assaulted and it leaves a mark, or causes mental cruelty (Children Act, 2004).

Pre-birth child protection conference:

If professionals consider an unborn baby to be at risk of significant harm, it may be decided to convene a pre-birth child protection conference. That will ensure there is a plan in place for when the child is born.

Primary carer: The primary carer may be either parent, grandparent, foster carer, or someone else. The primary carer is the one who provides the majority of the day-to-day care of the child.

Serious Case Reviews: As set out in *Working Together to Safeguard Children* (Department for Education 2010), a serious case review will always take place whenever a child dies, and there is thought to be an aspect of abuse, or neglect. There may also be a serious case review when a child has suffered serious injury through abuse or neglect, when a child has been seriously harmed as a result of being sexually abused, when a parent has been murdered and a domestic homicide review is initiated or a child has been seriously injured following a violent assault by another child or an adult *and* there are concerns about how individuals and/or agencies have worked together.

The Local Safeguarding Children Board (LSCB) is responsible for conducting the serious case review.

The main purpose of a serious case review is to examine what has happened and to try to learn lessons, to improve practice.

Section 17, Children Act, 1989: When *social care* is working with a family, they will be doing so either under s.47 of the Children Act, 1989, or s.17. The definition of s.47 is set out below, i.e. a child in need of protection. s.17 of the Act refers to children who are 'failing to thrive'. If that is the case, the Local Authority has a responsibility to provide services where the health and development of children are being avoidably impaired. Children who come under s.17 are often defined as 'Children in need'. s.17 is where there is a lower level of concern.

Section 47, Children Act, 1989: The Local Authority has a statutory duty to make enquiries where it has reasonable cause to suspect a child is suffering, or is likely to suffer significant harm. This is s.47 of the Children Act, 1989. In other words, s.47 is when it is believed a child is being abused, or neglected.

'Section 47' Investigation: Social workers talk about 'doing a Section 47 investigation'. This is an investigation under s.47, Children Act, 1989. As set out above, s.47 places a statutory duty on the Local Authority to make enquiries where it has reasonable cause to suspect a child is suffering, or is likely to suffer significantly. This can also be known as a 'child protection investigation'.

Service user:

Again, different professionals have different terms for their clients and different words go in and out of fashion. Currently social care talk about 'Service Users', meaning the families they are working with and this is the term used in this book.

Sexual abuse:

"Sexual abuse involves forcing or enticing a child or young person to take part in sexual activities, not necessarily involving a high level of violence, whether or not the child is aware of what is happening.

The activities may involve physical contact, including assault by penetration (e.g. rape or oral sex) or non-penetrative acts such as masturbation, kissing, rubbing and touching outside of clothing. They may include non-contact activities, such as involving children in looking at, or in the production of, sexual images, watching sexual activities, encouraging children to behave in sexually inappropriate ways, or grooming a child in preparation for abuse (including via the internet). Sexual abuse is not solely perpetrated by adult males. Women can also commit acts of sexual abuse, as can other children."

Working Together to Safeguard Children, 2010.

Sharing information:

There is much confusion about when and whether to share information about families. Best practice would say that we would have the family's permission to share information with other agencies, however, in terms of child protection, it is not a requirement. Legally we talk about sharing information if it is in the 'public interest', and what that means for us working in child protection is where there is a clear likelihood that a child is suffering, or is likely to suffer significant harm, agencies should be sharing relevant information, regardless of whether they have the family's permission to do so. Child protection overrides data protection and the human rights of the adults.

If social care is working under s.47 of the Children Act, 1989 permission does not have to be sought, or given. If we are working under s.17, we cannot share information without parental consent.

One of the common themes arising from serious case reviews is that agencies are not good at sharing information and information tends to be shared when it is too late, when the child has died. Unfortunately, we will never reach the point where we will be able to prevent every child from dying from abuse or neglect but there is no doubt we would do a better job at protecting children if we shared information before it is too late.

All you have to remember is: all agencies have to share information if they are undertaking a child protection investigation, or working with a child under s.47 of the Children Act, 1989.

Significant harm:

The Children Act, 1989, introduced the concept of significant harm as 'The threshold which justifies compulsory intervention in family life in the best interest of children. The Local Authority has a statutory duty to make enquiries where it has reasonable cause to suspect a child is suffering, or is likely to suffer significant harm' (Section 47).

Social care:

For the purpose of this book 'social care' refers to those working in the social work departments of Local Authorities. It is confusing that to different professionals the term has different meanings. To the government, 'social care' appears only to refer to adult services, whereas those of us working in children's services refer to ourselves working in 'social care'. The term 'Social Services' is also still used by some.

Strategy Discussion:

As set out in *Working Together to Safeguard Children, 2010* (Department of Education 2010), when a referral is made to *social care*, if it is thought to be a child protection case, the Local Authority's social care department has a duty to hold a strategy discussion involving police, health, social care and 'other bodies as appropriate, in particular the referring agency'. The purpose of the discussion is to decide on the next course of action.

Notes

INTRODUCTION

1 Available at: https://www.education.gov.uk/publications/standard/publicationDetail/Page1/CM%205730.
2 Available at: http://media.education.gov.uk/assets/files/pdf/s/second%20serious%20case%20overview%20report%20relating%20to%20peter%20connelly%20dated%20march%202009.pdf.
3 A serious case review should always be undertaken when a child dies and abuse or neglect is known or suspected to be a factor in the death (Department for Education 2010). There are other criterias, which are set out in "Working Together to Safeguard Children, 2010".

1 PREPARING FOR THE VISIT

1 There are national and may also be local confidential translator services.
2 Haringey LSCB Serious Case Review, Baby Peter, see http://www.haringeylscb.org.

3 GETTING IN THE DOOR

1 Khyra Ishaq's Serious Case Review, see http://www.lscbbirmingham.org.uk/downloads/Case+14.pdf.
2 http://www.ukba.homeoffice.gov.uk/while-in-uk/rightsandresponsibilities/publicfunds/.

4 WHAT TO LOOK OUT FOR

1 http://www.cheshireeastlscb.org.uk/images/library/files/SCR_CE001_Executive_Summary_for_publication_21st_July_2011.pdf.

5 KEEPING YOURSELF SAFE

1 Health and Safety Executive, see www.hse.gov.uk.
2 http://www.google.co.uk/url?sa=t&source=web&cd=1&ved=0CBsQFjAA&url=http%
3A%2F%2Fwww.ofsted.gov.uk%2Fnews%2Fvoice-of-child-learning-lessons-serious-
case-reviews-0&ei=GzBvTpfbCdOKhQeokfS0CQ&usg=AFQjCNGz3tsF_lv03WcK-
QssvrvJnAusiEQ; and http://www.google.co.uk/url?sa=t&source=web&cd=3&ved=0C
CoQFjAC&url=http%3A%2F%2Feducation.gov.uk%2Fpublications%2FeOrdering
Download%2FDFE-RR037.pdf&ei=cjBvTvu6IMWwhQeLxrXTCQ&usg=AFQjCN
FYPSCFNtwM-uIPOPVmTRTVkvS_gA.

Further reading and resources

The list of further reading and resources below is designed to provide a range of signposts to expand your knowledge base across the various areas considered. This is divided into different areas to help you to quickly identify the information you need.

KEEPING YOURSELF UP TO DATE

One of the key elements that you need to consider in child protection is the maintenance of your own knowledge and skills. As a social worker you are expected to have a detailed knowledge of your area, and the evidence which supports different interventions and outcomes. This knowledge can be difficult to maintain up to date in rapidly changing services and structures, and so it is important that you consider how you are going to sustain your competence and ensure that your practice is evidence-based. Books, magazines, journals and research reports are widely available and you will need to consider which formats you prefer to access information.

The internet is a valuable resource for social workers as it gives you instant access to a diverse range of information and contacts. Many written publications are also available, and regular press can also help you to maintain your knowledge base and ensure your recommendations are based on the most up to date evidence available.

These resources will help to get you started when you are newly qualified and help you to both improve your practice and to keep yourself abreast of developments across the social work profession as you continue your career.

The following resources are organisations/publications that will help to keep you informed. They will include a range of information that will provide the foundation of more detailed reading where necessary.

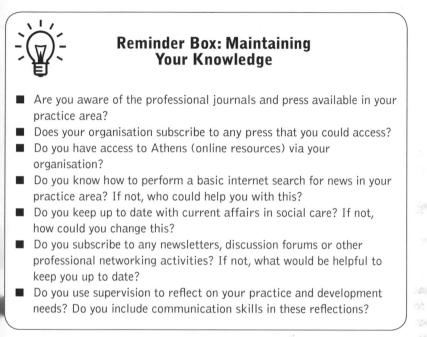

Reminder Box: Maintaining Your Knowledge

- Are you aware of the professional journals and press available in your practice area?
- Does your organisation subscribe to any press that you could access?
- Do you have access to Athens (online resources) via your organisation?
- Do you know how to perform a basic internet search for news in your practice area? If not, who could help you with this?
- Do you keep up to date with current affairs in social care? If not, how could you change this?
- Do you subscribe to any newsletters, discussion forums or other professional networking activities? If not, what would be helpful to keep you up to date?
- Do you use supervision to reflect on your practice and development needs? Do you include communication skills in these reflections?

RESOURCES

- Specific forums for children's social work practice can be found on CareSpace http://www.communitycare.co.uk/carespace/forums/default. aspx.
- *Children and Young People Now* is another magazine that you can access online. It also makes available all the latest news, research and best practice for those working in social care and other related professions. Access is limited unless a fee is paid: www.cypnow.co.uk.
- *Community Care* is the online trade magazine for social care practitioners. It includes articles, research updates, practice forums and links to discussion forums for social workers on many different issues: www.communitycare.co.uk.

■ Social care Online is a searchable database of social care publications, knowledge and research reviews provided by the social care Institute for Excellence (SCIE). They describe themselves as having the 'UK's most complete range of information and research on all aspects of social care': www.scie-socialcareonline.org.uk.

A number of organisations publish research and practice in this field, including the NSPCC (www.nspcc.org.uk) and Ofsted (www.ofsted.gov.uk).
  Other sites that will be useful for all types of practice include:

■ The Children's Workforce Development Council, www.cwdc.org.uk/. Includes a wide range of competency, development, and practice guidance across children and young people's social work.
■ NSPCC professionals website: http://www.nspcc.org.uk/Inform/ informhub_wda49931.html. Includes a range of information and news concerning safeguarding children, as well as resources and research information.
■ Research into serious case reviews is published by the Department for Education and can be found on their website: www.education.gov.uk. Ofsted also publishes serious case review data.
■ The report of the Munro Review of Child Protection (Munro 2011) includes some key findings and practice implications: https://www. education.gov.uk/publications/standard/Childrenandfamilies/Page1/ CM%208062.
■ The college of social work www.collegeofsocialwork.org

LEGISLATION AND STATUTORY GUIDELINES

Most of the legislation, and statutory guidelines, that you are likely to need is available on the internet. These are the key websites that will provide you with a comprehensive range of documents and resources to inform your practice.

■ Department for Education website: www.education.gov.uk. Publishes a range of policy, practice guidance, statutory guidance and government papers regarding children, young people and education.

- Legislation Online: www.legislation.gov.uk. Publishes Acts of Parliament, statutory instruments and ministerial orders across the UK.
- Your employer will have policies and procedures on employee safety and lone working, however, for the national perspective and legislation, details can be found through the Health and Safety Executive: ww.hse.gov.uk.

PROFESSIONAL STANDARDS

Social work is carried out in accordance with codes of practice and these should underpin all your practice activities: GSCC – www.gscc.org.uk; HPC – www.hpc-uk.org.

The Social Work Reform Board (SW Taskforce, 2009) set out recommendations about the professional structure of social work, and this has led to the establishment of The College of Social Work. Information is available on the College website and social workers can sign up to be prospective members: www.education.gov.uk/swrb and www.collegeofsocialwork.org.

FURTHER READING

Baron-Cohen, S. (2011) *Zero Degrees of Empathy: A New Theory of Human Cruelty.* London: Allen Lane.

Batmanghelidjh, C. (2007) *Shattered Lives: Children Who Live with Courage and Dignity.* London: Jessica Kingsley Publishers.

Howe, D. (2005) *Child Abuse and Neglect: Attachment, Development and Intervention.* Basingstoke: Palgrave Macmillan.

Ward, H., Brown, R., Westlake, D. and Davies, C. (2012) *Safeguarding Babies and Very Young Children from Abuse and Neglect (Safeguarding Children Across Services).* London: Jessica Kingsley Publishers.

References

Ainsworth, M.D.S. (1968) Object relations, dependency, and attachment: A theoretical review of the infant–mother relationship. *Child Development*, 40: 969–1025.

Ainsworth, M.D.S., Bell, S.M., and Stayton, D. (1974) Infant-mother attachment and social development. In M. P. Richards (ed.) *The Introduction of the Child into a Social World*. Cambridge: Cambridge University Press, pp. 99–135.

Bowlby, J. (1951) *Maternal Care and Mental Health*. Geneva: World Health Organization.

Braithwaite, R. (n.d.) *Guide to How to Deal with Hostile and Aggressive Adults or Young People and How to Manage Intimidating Situations*. Available at: www.ccinform.co.uk.

Brandon, M., Bailey, S. and Belderson, P. (2009) *Serious Case Reviews: A Two-Year Analysis of Child Protection Database Notifications 2007–2009*. Research Report DFE-RR040. London: DfE.

Department for Education (2010) *Working Together to Safeguard Children: A Guide to Inter-agency Working to Safeguard and Promote the Welfare of Children*. London: DfE.

Ferguson, H. (2009) Performing child protection: home visiting, movement and the struggle to reach the abused child, *Child and Family Social Work*, 14(4): 471–80.

London Borough of Brent (1985) *A Child in Trust: Report of the Panel of Inquiry into the Circumstances Surrounding the Death of Jasmine Beckford*. London: Borough of Brent.

Munro, E. (2010) *The Munro Review of Child Protection Part One: A Systems Analysis*. London: DfE.

Munro, E. (2011) *The Munro Review of Child Protection: Final Report: A Child-Centred System*. Available at: https://www.education.gov.uk/publications/standard/Childrenandfamilies/Page1/CM%208062.

Reder, P., Duncan, S. and Gray, M. (1993) *Beyond Blame: Child Abuse Tragedies Revisited*, London: Routledge.

Index

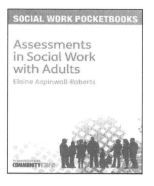

ASSESSMENTS IN SOCIAL WORK WITH ADULTS

Elaine Aspinwall-Roberts

9780335245215 (Paperback)
May 2012

eBook also available

This accessible survival guide shows social workers how to make their assessments the best, most effective and person-centred they can be.

Part of a new Social Work Pocketbooks series, the book is friendly, non-patronising and realistic about the day-to-day difficulties and challenges associated with assessing adults. It encourages you to reflect on how you work, and what you bring to the task.

Key features:

- Practical examples, advice and tips, including dealing with pitfalls
- Good practice and point of law reminders
- Fresh ideas on how to develop your assessment skills with adults

www.openup.co.uk

OPEN UNIVERSITY PRESS
McGraw · Hill Education

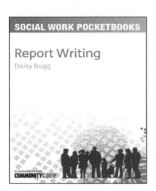

REPORT WRITING

Daisy Bogg

9780335245130 (Paperback)
May 2012

eBook also available

Report writing is a key social work skill, and one in which many practitioners receive very little formal training and preparation.

Part of a new Social Work Pocketbooks series published in association with Community Care, this easy to use guide will assist you in producing professional, informative and good quality reports. It provides key information, hints and tips to help you to develop your report writing style and to consider best practice in your written communication.

Key features:

- A range of report templates
- Examples of good practice in report writing
- Specialist chapters covering legal, policy and assessment situations

www.openup.co.uk

OPEN UNIVERSITY PRESS
McGraw · Hill Education

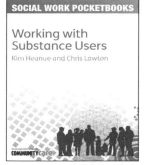

Working with Substance Users

Kim Heanue and Chris Lawton

9780335245192 (Paperback)
2012

eBook also available

This book, part of the Pocketbook series, will be a useful tool not only for experienced professionals but also newly qualified social workers and students. It deals with topics such as why people take substances and the risks involved as well as suggesting ways to deal with challenging situations.

Key features:

- A practical desk guide for social workers to refer to on a day-to-day basis.

www.openup.co.uk

OPEN UNIVERSITY PRESS
McGraw · Hill Education